Economic fallacies in Mizoram

Orange Books Publication

1st Floor, Rajhans Arcade, Mall Road, Kohka, Bhilai, Chhattisgarh 490020

Website: **www.orangebooks.in**

© Copyright, 2024, Author

All rights reserved. No part of this book may be reproduced, stored in a retrieval system, or transmitted, in any form by any means, electronic, mechanical, magnetic, optical, chemical, manual, photocopying, recording or otherwise, without the prior written consent of its writer.

First Edition, 2024

ISBN: 978-93-6554-003-1

ECONOMIC FALLACIES IN
MIZORAM

LALHRUAIZELA FANAI

OrangeBooks Publication
www.orangebooks.in

Table of Contents

1. Introduction — 1
2. Tribalism in Mizoram — 7
   - Culture — 9
   - Assimilation — 11
   - Economics — 15
   - Summary — 16
3. The Dunning-Kruger Effect in Economics — 17
4. The Demonisation of Greed — 21
   - Questioning the Essentiality of Essential Goods and Services — 26
   - The Price of Moral Constraints — 28
5. Misplaced Priorities — 29
   - Wasteful Spending on Human Resources — 43
6. Fallacies Around Inequality — 44
   - Wealth Redistribution — 47
   - Fictional Wealth — 49
   - Debunking the Arguments Against Growth — 52
7. A Belief that Government is the Economy — 55
8. The Strong Government Fallacy — 58
   - Regulation — 61
9. Fallacies Around Inflation — 64
   - Land Price Inflation — 67
10. The Illusion Of Price Control — 70
    - Tenancy Rates — 77
11. The Sustainable Economy Fallacy — 79
12. The Greedy Banker Fallacy — 81
13. The Inner Line Permit Fallacy — 84

14.	**Fallacies Around a Planned Economy**	**88**
	➢ Bringing Opportunity Cost into the Equation	90
15.	**The Effects of a Centralised Education**	**92**
	➢ The Dangers of Education for All	97
16.	**The Keynesian Havoc**	**100**
	➢ Even After Keynesian, the Market is King	105
17.	**Fear of Financial Instruments, but Investing in Pyramid Schemes**	**107**
18.	**A Misconception on Value**	**110**
	➢ A Misunderstanding of Money	113
	➢ A Misunderstanding of Profit	117
19.	**Fallacies Surrounding Big Corporates**	**120**
20.	**The Incorrect Assumption that Morality and Economic Soundness are Similar**	**124**
21.	**The Economics of Theft**	**127**
	➢ The Risks and Rewards of Theft	129
	➢ The Economics of Corruption	131
	➢ Reducing Corruption	133
	➢ The Black Market	136
22.	**The Fallacy of Scale**	**142**
23.	**Fallacies Surrounding Entrepreneurship**	**144**
24.	**The Scrooges of Christmas**	**152**
25.	**The Evils of the Anointed**	**154**
26.	**Press Freedom and Democracy**	**156**
27.	**Fallacies Around Agriculture**	**158**
28.	**Conclusion**	**160**
29.	**Bibliography**	**162**

1

Introduction

With the advent of the internet and social media that came along with it, Mizoram has seen a meteoric rise in discussions about economic development. These discussions have also significantly impacted the governance and decision-making processes of politicians. As a result, there have been reversals in the decisions taken by politicians regarding specific strategies.

I attribute the cause of this to the quick dissemination of information among the people due to improvement in information technology. As a result, there is now a more direct influence of the people on governance. This influence is evident during the ordinary course of the tenure of a ruling party. It has now become even more crucial to examine the economic conditions without bias, based on well-established economic principles, so as to put a correct perspective into these deliberations.

Economic analyses that present only statistics and data without providing an in-depth analysis is difficult to understand for the common people. Economics as a discipline is incomplete without the understanding of why humans behave the way they do, and any attempt to divert economic science from the innate human nature and replace them with ideologies is not just wrong, but also dangerous.

This book tries to differentiate itself from many of the books on economics. It outlines different challenges within the state of Mizoram, highlights the people's general beliefs, and punctuates the common fallacies of these beliefs that may exist using well-established economic principles. In order to make it palatable for the readers, I shall try to avoid citing too many statistics in my deliberations, and instead rely on the principles, the evidence that is easily visible to everyone and the conclusions that well-renowned economists and intellectuals have arrived at while providing the validity of my claims.

Mizoram is one of the smaller states in India, covering roughly 21000 square kilometers. It has a population of around 12 lakh people and a limited domestic production of around Rs. 32829.46 crore during 2022-23.

There is a general belief among the residents that the state needs to live up to its full potential for several decades. This public displeasure is evident in different forms of media and conversations among the residents. It also appears to be a consensus among the people that the government can perform exponentially better and that corruption, be it moral or monetary, is the root cause of the slow pace of development.

A discourse on the poor quality of education is also common. There are complaints about the low quality of the infrastructure built by the government. The people also yearn for a solid hand to quash the rampant corruption and societal evils. Greed is also pinned as an evil plaguing society, especially among the traders.

Since Christianity is the main religion of the residents by an overwhelming margin, the people opine that the various evils in society are caused by the lack of true devotion to their faith. A large section of the people regard the minorities and mainlander residents, traders, and bureaucrats as threats to their existence and that assimilation is an ever-present danger. The ever-increasing number of traders, laborers, and professionals entering the state is perceived to be the beginning of an impending doom to the purity of the Mizo tribe, and it also hurts the residents economically. This perceived threat is a source of discontent among the general populace, making it an essential point of consideration for political strategies. There have also been border disputes with the neighboring states, adding fuel to these sentiments.

The GSDP of Mizoram mainly depends on the service sector and public utilities. The contribution from the secondary sector is minimal and primarily based on public consumption of necessities such as electricity, natural gas, etc. In contrast, the primary sector, which provides more than 50% of the employment, is not a significant contributor to the state's domestic product, which shows that there is still a substantial dependency on agriculture population-wise. Still, the overall income from agriculture is low, indicating that poverty plagues a large number of people within the population. Moreover, the payment of the service sector is mainly dependent on the government, which highlights a deficiency of organic growth in the sector.

There is no doubt that the people of Mizoram want a good government, a fast-paced development, a productive workforce and an honest society.

However, good intentions do not guarantee good results.

The public needs to be properly guided on at the very least, the basic principles of economics so that they do not commit fallacies while making their demands from the legislature. Hence, I shall try to be as clear as possible while explaining why good intentions can lead to bad outcomes while citing evidence and also, analyze our general beliefs and the reason behind the situation that we are in at present using basic principles of economics.

I firmly hold the belief that no country contains a group of citizens that deliberately try to derail their own country. An economic or a political collapse happens when people fail to see the overall effects of their decisions on a large scale, as the effects of personal decisions or interest groups often have a very different effect on a larger scale such as a state or a country.

Societies perform very well while dealing with anti-social behaviours that are on the edge of the spectrum such as rape, torture, or murder. Problems occur when society tries to deal with subjective qualities such as greed, honesty, altruism, patriotism, fairness and of course, the favorite of the social justice warriors; equality. These topics often form the basis of discussions as many people fervently try to convince the general public, and have even largely succeeded. One success of this is the existence of a strong cohesion among the Mizo people living within and outside Mizoram. There is also a strong fear of outsiders as assimilation is considered to be a threat to the purity of the Mizo tribe. Big businesses are feared and their entry into Mizoram is considered to be a threat for the small businesses. There were protests to prevent railway connectivity. The Mizo people also often complain about the increase in the number of outsiders who have settled within Mizoram. They complain that the moral corruption of the people who enable these outsiders to settle within Mizoram is the reason for this so-called problem.

The main problem with these discussions is that although the intentions of the people are mostly pure, they often overlook evidence. Human history is full of ripe resources to determine which opinion is true or false, and to confine it to the subject of this book, which economic decisions are sound and which are detrimental for the people. When a policy is not aligned with the innate nature of human beings, it produces undesirable results elsewhere even when the objectives are achieved.

An evaluation that does not look at the tradeoff is often dangerous.

A real problem emerges when the artificial problems that are generated from planned actions are more pernicious than the original problem, as everyone is usually clueless on how to solve that new problem, let alone realise the actual reason why that problem has emerged in the first place. Socialist principles also tend to be riddled with noble ideas that are often very appealing to politicians and the people. However, a very different picture emerges when we look at the results. We often have intellectuals who have an idea for the perfect solution to all our problems, but these intellectuals actually never know how that idea would be implemented, and what would be the cost. Any suggestion must have a complete set of necessary facts to implement the idea.

Economic fallacies are common all around the globe. Various schools of economics have highlighted these fallacies based on their own theories. Unfortunately, I have discovered that the same fallacies plague the people of Mizoram. Addressing these fallacies is crucial to prevent people from driving their representatives in the wrong direction. This book tries to bring the beliefs that are thought to be common knowledge in economic science, but are actually false when looked at closely. The cost of holding these beliefs is high, but sadly, people tend to ignore the data and hold a belief system that is based on faith.

2

Tribalism in Mizoram

While culture and society does not fall strictly under the discipline of economics, it has a large effect on the economic decisions of the people, and thus it cannot be ignored. Therefore, I shall try to briefly correlate the effects of the culture of the Mizos with the economics in Mizoram.

Humans existed as small tribes for a long time. A hostility towards outsiders is ingrained into our animal instincts, and is therefore not unique to the Mizos. This hostility is the reason for conflicts, wars and many other ugly things mankind has done, and is continuing today. The level of hostility towards outsiders is not the same for different cultures. Cultures that have a lesser amount of exposure to the outside world invariably tend to have higher levels of insecurity towards outside influence. This can be understood as an extension of the appreciation a person has for herself, to the society or the culture in which that person was brought up in. When a society has lesser interaction with outsiders, this appreciation is not extended to that outsider, for which the reasons may be unfamiliarity with the facial or body features, habits, culture or language. Moreover, due to the lesser connection with outside societies, this type of society also has a lesser incentive to assimilate into other cultures.

Culture

Like other cultures, the Mizo people are biased, and have a certain conceitedness towards their own culture. The Mizo people have a general perception that their culture is the best in the world as it is theirs, and that they must preserve it at all costs. They perceive outside influences as negative, and they try their best to insulate their society from it. They also like to impress upon the community to popularize clothes that preserve the Mizo culture, especially for the women. They regard any change in the status quo as a threat to the continued existence of the Mizos, if that change is not towards the strengthening of what they believe to be the Mizo cultural traits.

However, what exactly constitutes Mizo culture is more or less arbitrary and is subject to the interpretation of the person defining it. When Mizo women marry outside the community, they are seen as traitors. At the same time, Mizos give a certain level of exception when a male marries outside his community, as the Mizo customary law accepts the descendants from the male side to be a Mizo, while the descendants of a female Mizo with a non-Mizo spouse are not. This customary practice does not appear logical, as even if the characteristics of the offspring are not exactly equally shared from both parents, totally discrediting the contribution of either parent appears to be fallacious.

Lately, the Mizo people have become increasingly aware of the small size of their population, and there is a considerable discussion about the need to increase the Mizo population. The churches are now also involved by offering incentives to the families who have children. This sentiment is strengthened by the empowerment provided by the internet, which allows for easier discussions among cohesive groups.

Assimilation

The Mizos also fear assimilation. This fear seems to be rooted in the misunderstanding of the true nature of assimilation, and the history of the human race. First, let us look at what assimilation actually means.

The Mizos seem to think that assimilation means destruction, rather than the actual meaning used by social scientists, which is 'to become similar'.

The ease of assimilation among races has many factors, such as similarities with respect to religion, facial features, language, history, social practices, general sentiment towards the foreign cultures, etc. Social scientists would not attribute a negative or a positive connotation to the word assimilation, but would only make particular attributions with respect to particular topics. In general, different races tend to bond more easily when they assimilate easily, which can be regarded as positive, but this is exactly opposite to the general understanding of the Mizo people.

It is true that during the process of assimilation, some parts of the cultures will be transformed, which appears to be the fear of the Mizo people. However, it is important to understand that even in the absence of other assimilating influences, cultures evolve continuously. A person born today would have a completely different experience from her parents. If a Mizo from the past looked at the culture of the Mizo people today, she would see a completely different culture. Thus, it would benefit the Mizo people to shift their focus from merely preserving what exists, to adopting practices that are good for the future.

One fallacy that most Mizos believe is that sharing of living space automatically leads to assimilation. While this notion carries its merits, as the interaction of cultures would induce at least some level of mutual absorption on both sides, it is not always the case among different cultures.

The Jews were removed from their homeland and were scattered across different parts of the globe. However, they retained their identity wherever they settled.

The Tibetans have also retained their identity even after staying for many years in India.

The Mizos retain their identity even in Delhi, where they are vastly outnumbered by other cultures.

The Gorkhas have retained a distinct identity to a great extent even after living with the Mizos for many years.

On the other hand, the Mizos continue to be deeply influenced by the British, even though they left many decades ago. The dress code of the Mizos today is derived from the Europeans. The religion of the Mizos is also largely influenced by that of the British.

Lately, the Mizo youth has been deeply influenced by Korean pop culture, even though physical interaction is more or less absent. The Mizos copy the clothes, music and even culinary tastes from the Korean stars.

An interesting phenomenon that I have observed is that many daily wage laborers from the neighboring states, who had started entering Mizoram many decades ago, do not have much cultural influence on the Mizos. These laborers, who mostly belong to the Hindu or Muslim religion, do not influence the Mizos to adopt their religion, or to adopt their cultural practices. Inter-marriage is also mostly non-existent. They instead tend to adopt Mizo culture and sometimes Christianity, but not the other way around. Hence, the adoption of cultural and religious practices in this case is mostly unidirectional.

I have shown that the intermingling of races does not directly lead to proper assimilation, and the physical separation of the races does not prevent assimilation either. It is dependent on many factors and hence, the general view that the Mizos have towards assimilation requires a revision.

The genetic purity of Mizos also appears to be a concern. They believe that mixing Mizo blood with other races would lead to the loss of the Mizo identity. This view is not just problematic in many ways, but it is also unscientific. Humans have been interbreeding for thousands of years. Evolutionary scientists often point out that many people still have neanderthal genes, who are the cousins of homo- sapiens. It has also already been established that Mizos are simply one of the many mongoloid races. To take things further, genetic diversity improves a species, instead of weakening it, which completely destroys the racial purity argument. Scientists often face problems while trying to repopulate endangered species of animals due to inbreeding. Therefore, trying to establish a racial purity for a small sub-tribe, who are descendants of a long chain of different human tribes does not carry any meaning, nor does it confer any benefit to the Mizo people. It is also impractical to allow the intermingling of different races as it can lead to many problems. The aim should be to develop a practical method so that the benefits of free inter-state movement can be utilised, while preventing problems that can occur due to racial and cultural conflicts. Ideally, the number of people who permanently migrate into Mizoram should be not more than a rate that can be organically assimilated into the society.

Economics

Most of the people that have come to Mizoram tend to have economic reasons. They believe that these outsiders have a hidden agenda, while these people are simply moving into Mizoram due to economic opportunities. Wages are higher than most of the other states due to various reasons, but it appears to be mainly due to a higher tax devolution from the Central Government. Low skilled jobs are also in high demand. This has led to an influx of low skilled workers who try to make a living. Non-Mizos have also tried to set up businesses, despite restrictions placed upon them by the Inner Line Permit system. These influxes are seen as a threat to the safety of the Mizo people, as they fear assimilation, and by assimilation, they often mean being taken over. Examples of indigenous people being overtaken by foreigners are often cited as examples, but are often generalised. A closer look around the world reveals that immigration is not a simple matter of taking over the weaker race. There is a complex mechanism that is based on geography, conflict, culture, skin colour, food or history. We also commit an open ended fallacy, which means that the outsiders will infinitely move into Mizoram. This reasoning is flawed, as most of the influx is due to economic reasons, and the influx would cease as soon as the incentive is neutralised. This neutralisation of incentive will come mainly in the form of reduced wages with respect to the neighbouring states.

Summary

While it is important to open up the economy for economic growth, the Mizos tend to believe that opening up the economy would lead to their downfall. Mizoram as a state has a certain distinctiveness in the sense that the Mizo identity is concocted with the state of Mizoram. They also hold the false belief that what has worked for other states will not work for them as they are special and unique. Some of them are also waiting on the divine to show them the way. This has successfully driven the Mizoram people to block all outsiders without analysing the pros and cons. They also commit a fallacy called open ended fallacy by believing that inward movement into Mizoram will continue indefinitely, which is clearly limited by the number of easily available jobs. However, they are correct in the sense that a quick influx of outsiders moving into Mizoram can cause problems, and prevent successful assimilation. The finer details of this issue are left for the social scientists of Mizoram to tackle. What this book mainly tries to outline is that every decision includes a trade-off, which may or may not be desirable. The Mizo people cannot commit the mistake of taking a decision without realising that there is a trade-off for this important decision. Thus, this issue, just like any other issue, requires a careful analysis and the Mizo people must avoid knee-jerk emotional reactions.

3

The Dunning-Kruger Effect in Economics

When a person's lack of knowledge and skill in a certain area causes them to overestimate their own competence, it is called the Dunning Kruger effect. This phenomenon is observable across all disciplines, but I have found it to be much more prevalent within the field of economic science. We have a substantial number of people who are sure that they know how to make Mizoram rich, but are unable to grow the wealth for themselves. People comfort themselves by using lines like 'No one can predict the future, least of all economists'. They fail to see the difference between making a prediction and following the well-established economic principles. Due to this, people often tend to rely on their opinions instead of looking closely at the research of well-read experts. Economists, like any other expert in other fields, have committed blunders, and will continue to do so. Committing mistakes teaches us to make advances in any field. When mistakes are committed, we can move away from the wrong assumptions and refine our opinions, and it does not reduce the credibility of the field.

One of the reasons why people tend to have a disbelief in economics is that whatever mistakes are committed are easily visible to the common man. Evidence for this was seen during covid pandemic. People working in the field of medicine had to make worldwide announcements while the research was still underway. Since these announcements were the result of their recent studies, they were improved upon, or even at times, retracted. This aroused a considerable amount of suspicion among the masses, who had previously remained largely oblivious to the scientific process that had always been followed by researchers. The people asked, "If science keeps on changing, why should we believe it?". This seems logical to the otherwise uninitiated. However, the uninteresting truth is that scientists are just debaters, who debate using evidence and logic. What is being followed is simply the scientific opinion that has the best evidence in support of it. Like other people around all parts of the globe, this is very difficult to accept for most of the Mizo people, who are deeply religious with strong dogmatic beliefs. For people like them, when any part of a discipline is disproved, it means the dismantlement of the entire field. Thus, it is quite natural that in a field like economics where people are tuned in to the work of the experts, as it affects them directly, there is a general suspicion around the subject as they cannot differentiate between works that are on the frontier which could later be improved or even disproved, to the well-established theories that have been proven to withstand the test of time. Combine this with the propensity of people to believe their own opinions instead of the input provided by others, even when the input is provided by an expert, then we have fertile grounds for the Dunning Kruger effect to take place.

The stubbornness of the people, who do not believe in the words of the experts, has led them to hold opinions about what is good for Mizoram, opinions that are often untrue and at times, directly contradict well established economic principles. These beliefs reverberate through the society and invariably, incorporated into public administration by the Legislators. When these policies are actually implemented and their impact is felt, the same people who had advocated for the policies tend to blame the politicians and the bureaucrats.

For example, people say that things are more expensive in Mizoram because of the greed of the shopkeepers, while a simple application of the principles of economics would show that things are expensive because there is less competition and the market for business is also small in Mizoram, which is a direct consequence of the implementation of the inner line permit system, which is held so dearly by the people who make these allegations.

While we discuss the fallacies that the people commit, we must also point to the fact that India has a lot of economists and bureaucrats from the left. There is a whole spectrum in the school of economics, from the Austrian, the Chicago style free market economists, the Keynesians to the modern monetary theorists. The Indian intellectuals and bureaucrats tend to stay politically correct and are careful not to stray too far to the right. The books on economics and even the syllabus for the recruitment of the bureaucrats are mostly based on government intervention on the economy. Thus, when people are very confident that they are stating the obvious, they are usually on the far left of the spectrum, which causes a deep imbalance in the economic policy of Mizoram, and also for the country as a whole.

4

The Demonization of Greed

'Of course, we are not greedy, the other guy is'

-Milton Friedman

People like to attribute the cause of various social evils to greed. It is simplistic and convincing. But, even if greed were a demon, we still need an accurate idea of solving the problem. People love to discuss the evils of crony capitalism and its ill effects on society. The citizens blame the businessmen for being greedy, and they blame them for engaging in price-gouging. People often fail to see that no particular group is particularly greedy. This misconception is likely to cause fallacies. The people's demands from policymakers are misguided by this over-simplified view of a complex emergent property of man's wants and desires.

Let us dissect what we call greed to understand it better. People often term greed as any type of superfluous want or desire. However, they often fail to see that 'superfluous' is subjective. What I call a necessity is a luxury for someone else. What I call development could be an irresponsible exploitation of natural resources in someone else's eyes.

A man who saves for old age is considered greedy by a carefree person.

A CEO who tries to achieve higher profit margins is a corporate scrooge for most people, but the shareholders of his company laud the success of the CEO's plan.

A politician who throws a fundraiser is a corrupt fellow who cares for nothing but winning an election, but that same politician is doing a noble deed for his group in dire need of campaign funds.

A charitable person who puts all his funds into charity trusts is considered greedy, as he is doing it to dodge taxes.

A beneficiary of a government scheme is also acting selfishly as he is already middle class.

A beneficiary of a compensation due to land acquisition is considered greedy by the anointed class, but it is his only chance of escaping poverty and he regards it as a blessing from God.

A shopkeeper who closes late and misses a church service is also greedy, but his action is noble for his kid, who needs new shoes.

So, to sum up," Greed lies in the eye of the beholder."

Economic development is brought about in two ways:

A. By adding value.

B. An increase in consumption, which in turn fuels production.

Value addition is the act of making something more valuable than its previous state. This increase in value due to human ingenuity adds to the aggregate wealth of a country or a state. Also, an increase in production tends to lower prices, boosting consumption. This increase in sales for the seller, complemented by the price drop for the consumer, leads to economic growth. Value addition due to human ingenuity is less guilty of producing waste than the increase in consumption. None the less, they both contribute to economic growth. This same principle applies to all other economic activities. They fuel economic growth irrespective of whether people consider the activities noble or greedy. Filtering the supposedly greedy activities would shave off the growth achieved from these activities.

For example, people may consider a shopkeeper who spends less time with his kids due to his business irresponsible and greedy. However, by spending less time at his shop, he would earn a lesser income. This lower income would also directly affect his family. His customers would also have to travel a longer distance or be unable to buy the products they need on time if he closes early, leading to economic losses. Thus, this economic loss has to be weighed against the loss in time spent with his kids. The simple fact is that it is impossible for a government or any single agency to determine what is best for all shopkeepers. Therefore, it is best that the choice is left to the shopkeepers. It becomes clear that lesser interference by agencies and society to individual decisions would lead to better economic growth.

Policymakers might want to remember this -
"One may be smarter than everyone, but one is never smarter than everyone combined."

The maximization of freedom of choice brings the best outcome in almost all instances. This is clearly visible when comparisons are made among various countries and ranking them by their economic freedom index. To judge other people's choices and term them as greedy is shortsighted at best. The real harm appears when groups of people tend to pressurize the government and enact laws to curb the supposed greed of other people. This simply restricts the freedom of choice and stifles innovation.

The ugly truth is that to grow a business into a large company, the business has had to achieve high profits at least once at some point of time. This high profit gives it the breathing space required for the acquisition of other businesses, attract equity or scale up its production which allows it to lower its prices and compete with other big players. The choking of this profit only prevents the growth of businesses in Mizoram, which lowers overall growth for the state.

One could argue that businesses can still achieve scale by the acquisition of debt or through the subscription of equity from investors. However, we have to keep in mind that businesses fail all the time. The losses incurred by these failed businesses that were propped up by debt or investor's equity would still be paid in one form or another by society. Banks will have to write off their losses and investors will have to lower their spending due to these losses, causing an overall lowering of spending in the economy. Even if our central bank decides to put the money back into circulation, it will still be paid for it by the people in the form of inflation. There is no simple way to avoid this. Thus, it is best not to play God and leave the people to do their bidding with minimal interference.

Questioning the Essentiality of Essential Goods and Services

Mizo people are often guilty of signaling virtue when a businessman is engaged in a trade that affects a majority of the population; these are often the so-called essential commodities and other goods and services that are a common requirement for the people. Goods and services such as maxi cabs, taxis, buses, food items and clothing fall into this category. Restrictions are placed on these commercial items or services by appealing to its essentiality. These restrictions have positive effects such as affordability, a certain level of government control in times of crises and orientation of the services to the general public. However, these conveniences do not come free of cost. The advantages should be weighed with the disadvantages, such as low quality of service, prevention of the emergence of premium options for travelers, lack of safety features due to fixing of price etc. Ideally, the aim must be to utilise the best of both worlds to a maximum extent.

Somehow, the people feel that the normal freedom that is granted to the other businessmen should not be allowed as these are simply too important. However, the very restriction that is placed upon these goods and services prevents the formalisation of these businesses, thus preventing the exploitation of economies of scale, which keeps the prices of these goods and services relatively high. Therefore, it is crucial that we look at economic activities in terms of trade-offs and not directly assign our moral values to them.

Growth does not come free and there is a price for it. We either pay for it or we stunt economic growth.

The Price of Moral Constraints

The moral constraints that are placed upon the Mizo people due to the fallacy surrounding greed is substantial, and its ill- effects even larger.

The youth, full of zest, who already have a tendency to indulge in anti-social activities such as drugs, alcohol etc., quickly fall into the wrong path when their natural urge to compete or attain wealth and status are suppressed.

This is even more pronounced among males, the more competitive gender, which is not surprising. While people are quick to point to the cause of these problems as the work of the devil, a closer look reveals that moral constraints that prevent the youth from fulfilling their ambitions, changes in living standards, lack of responsibilities of boys in their households or the simple availability of the substances while society is still not equipped with the knowledge to protect itself against them look suspiciously more like the real causes. The Mizo youth are encouraged to follow their passion only when it comes to academic careers, sports or government jobs. This leaves a huge chunk of the youth to never attain success in the eyes of the society, no matter how much they attain in their careers.

5

Misplaced Priorities

While we discuss economic freedom, it is also important to look into the costs of misplaced priorities. This misplaced priority can be seen in many countries while they are trying to address their economic problems, and we also need to introspect. People often tend to blame the government for most of the social and economic ills that they are facing. We can say that this is mostly justified. However, the evidence shows that the solution is often not what we believe it to be. It is difficult to convince a group of people who are already convinced that they know the answer to the economic problems of Mizoram. I have assigned myself the duty to highlight these misplaced priorities, so that some light is shed into these fallacies.

While it must be apparent that the main role of a government is governance, we have a belief that a government's main job is to bring development and uplift the poor. Some economists of Mizoram also look at the budget and point to the lesser ratio of funds for development as a bad thing, while it is very obvious that the core function of a government is to provide governance, and not execute development projects. The analysis of these economists would only work if the cost of hiring people engaged in the execution of the development project itself is compared to the outcome of that project.

While providing security to the people and establishing a tort system that provides a fair playing ground to businesses or any other activity is of prime importance, we often focus on the provision of public services and aid to the people. It is not surprising that this mistake occurs, as it is quite counter intuitive. Any coherent person would easily conclude that something that is taken care of would fare better than something that has no care-taker. However, when it comes to the economy or raising children, some things are counter-intuitive, and demand a look at the outcome rather than winning the debates. Countries like Singapore or Hong Kong that were forced to adopt free trade policies have done well, while governments of many countries that have the power to make economic choices for the welfare of their citizens have ironically performed worse.

The deficiencies in the services provided by the government are often blamed on insufficient resources of the government, corruption or the incompetence of the bureaucrats and politicians. This type of thinking fails to look at the most important feature of a government, which is that any government is being run by people that have their own self-interests, who are looking after money that was not earned by them. This simple conflict of interest explains why corruption and inefficiencies are so common in any government. Looking at the real objectives of the bureaucrats and the politicians would reveal a very different picture from what is commonly perceived.

While a government is executing projects, it has many priorities that may not be apparent to the public. A government official, just like any human being, seeks to advance his career and make some kind of impact even if they refrain from engaging in direct corruption. The path to achieving that objective would be, in many cases, different from what the public wants from the government. A politician also has other motives that are not so visible; such as getting re-elected, or rewarding his campaigners for their hard-work and loyalty, among other things.

If we look at the hidden objectives, we can clearly see that a government is not so inefficient after all. The only catch is that it has other objectives that are not desired by the public.

We cannot stop a politician from campaigning or erase the innate desire of a bureaucrat. Hence, it must be accepted that inefficiency and corruption are part of the features of a government, however painful it may be. Even if we happen to have a group of bureaucrats and politicians who are completely selfless, ten others are in line looking to replace them at their first chance. Hence, the cry to elect a pious leader who would pull us out of the rubble is futile if we do not understand the reasons why government agencies act in the manner that they do.

More checks, stronger laws, harsher punishments and anti-corruption laws are the usual prescriptions from the anointed class. These prescriptions tend to increase government presence. While they have merits, they also tend to make the people somewhat docile.

Thus, the focus should be shifted on the alignment of the interest of the officials that hold the power to the desired objectives as much as possible.

Increasing check mechanisms only add more inefficiencies and more players to the corruption circle. That is why the role of a government is to provide a fair playing field to the participants of the economy, with minimal interference.

Instead of what is actually believed by most of the people, economists tend to point to the pendency of cases in Indian courts and over-regulation as major impediments for business growth as it creates uncertainty for businessmen, especially foreign investors. It may not be obvious to a left leaning person, but a careful quantification of the effects would show that the removal of this pendency would far outweigh many traditional development schemes where huge resources are allocated every year. While the case backlog issue may not be a particular problem to solve for Mizoram as a state, the cost of the Mizoram people allocating their attention to the wrong area has a negative impact on the economy.

Due to this wrong perception, the Mizoram people rarely demand an improvement on the business environment in Mizoram. Rather, they ask for new districts, new blocks or new government offices.

The cost of this misplaced attention has held the economic development back by at least a few years.

Reduction in the number of regulations, speedy disposal of cases in courts, quick arbitration and settlement of disputes in quasi-judicial bodies as well as out of court settlements are always of prime importance for the growth of the economy. It may also be pointed out that a strong court system tends to be superior when compared to the direct superintendence of the people by the government due to the simple fact that courts or quasi-courts cannot routinely directly issue directions to the people. The orders usually come as a result of the activation of these institutions by the aggrieved parties. Instead of placing our priority on hastening litigation to provide a fertile business environment or to restrict the courts from issuing blanket orders that render them to take the role of the executive, we place our priorities on these other things. There has not been much public pressure in India to increase the fora for litigation which has an enormous lag due to a large pendency of cases.

The relatively shorter arm of a judicial system provides more freedom to the people to make economic choices on their own.

This translates to better economic freedom for the people. At the same time, when people have the power to act on their own to solve their problems, it gives them a sense of pride and confidence. This is in contrast to direct superintendence over the citizens, which tends to remove the importance of the individual, and puts more focus on government agencies. This point may be understood by looking at the larger sphere of function of the courts in the United States, where even immigration and citizenship involve their judiciary.

The Mizo people, and also a large number of Indians, are placed at very high positions for the development of the country. The publishing of the results of recruitment into government services by the media commands a high level of attention. Countries that were once colonized by the British tend to have a civil service system that is organized, and India is one of such countries. However, even some developed countries like Singapore have a civil service structure that looks quite similar to the British era. Thus, to blame the civil service structure itself for the slower growth of India, and by extension, Mizoram, would be wrong. On the other hand, countries that do not have a civil structure similar to India, such as the United States or Canada also have a relatively high per capita income. Thus, the logical conclusion is that the type of civil service structure adopted by a country is not a determining factor in its economic fate. It appears that when bureaucrats are corrupt, it is merely a symptom of a larger problem.

A painful impact that is felt by Mizoram due to this misplaced priority is that the government has become very heavy. Like many other states in India, Mizoram has also felt severe financial hardships, which is often attributed to several causes like corruption, lack of expertise in public administration or finance, the greed of our politicians or even due to the lack of true faith in the Christian God. Pointing to these causes is easy, and they are easily agreed upon. Hence, public discussions tend to focus on these alleged causes. However, this fails to address the root cause of the overheated spending pattern that has been continuing for several decades in Mizoram. If we look closer, we would see that these so-called causes tend to look more like symptoms. This phenomenon is simply an emerging property which occurs due to the over-reliance of the people on the government, which is a classic trait of a socialist government. This shouldering of heavy responsibilities by the government, with all its inherent inefficiencies, tends to recruit more and more employees for its civil services, with a heavy weightage on the employees that work on development and the provision of social welfare services. Whatever ill befalls our society, the answer is usually to blame the government, which pushes the government to adopt more socialist traits. While this puts a strain on its financial resources, it also puts a strain on the government on the hiring of its essential workers such as the people engaged in medical professions, teachers, policemen, firefighters and judges. It can be said that these essential workers form the core of governance as even staunch capitalists seldom argue for the total privatization of these services.

Due to this misplaced priority, a peculiar situation has emerged where people have trouble accessing the most basic of a government service, such as a good road or swift access to justice, but are able to avail free internet.

Another fallacy that is common among educated people is that a good bureaucratic system is important for development. *Although personal experience provides an urge to say that bureaucracy often hinders growth, countries like China and Singapore have strong bureaucracies, yet they perform reasonably well economically. On the other hand, in countries like the USA or Canada, bureaucrats have a smaller role. Appointments of high-ranking officials in these countries are also not based on merit, but on political favors. Yet, these countries also perform well and are among the developed countries. So, the only logical conclusion is that bureaucracy is neither important nor a hindrance to economic development. However, all countries that have repressive regimes have strong bureaucracies in different forms, as these bureaucrats are the means through which the rulers exercise their powers.* Moreover, even in the developed countries that have strong bureaucracies, the citizens tend to have lesser social freedom, as in the case of China. Thus, to drive this point home, Mizoram should not prioritize its civil service to the point that the expenses become a burden for the government. Enough experimentation has been done to provide sufficient proof that privatization, outsourcing, right-sizing and public-private partnership modes can easily reduce the burden of the government while still providing essential services to its citizens.

Contrary to the common error of blaming the government for being corrupt, some people also tend to blame the society, which also proves to be untenable under the same logic that is discussed above.

Some bureaucrats even blame the citizens for wanting 'rights' without accepting the 'responsibilities'.

The blaming of the people on their supposed lack of morality, hard work or a lack of will to make sacrifices for the state is without evidence, and does not provide actionable points that appear achievable. While culture impacts the economy deeply, the inverse is also true. People living under harsh economic conditions tend to have lower inhibitions. This cannot be blamed on the people, as it is a biological impulse for survival. Evidence for this can be seen when we look at what appears to be a higher prevalence of criminal behaviour of the Mizo people from Myanmar where the people are facing a severe hardship. These people are believed to be genetically similar to the Mizo people living within Mizoram, but exhibit a vastly different behavior. This variation can only be attributed to the difference in the environment of these two groups of people.

Under the same vein, we could also argue that people who exhibit a lack of these supposed desirable traits as framed by the social justice activists are merely symptoms of a deeper underlying cause that require a closer look. While it may be impossible to study every individual, there are common traits that tend to emerge among people when exposed to certain environments. Thus, we may start the analysis for the identification of the traits that we find undesirable by looking at the current system that exists in Mizoram. We can look at different places and see where these systems also exist, and look at the impact on the people's traits. If a common trait develops under a similar system in other places, we may hypothesise that the reason for the emergence of that trait is the system.

Thus, simply saying that people lack ambition and are lazy is not helpful.

The discussion must be on what drives people to behave in the manner that they do, and point to actionable objectives to remove the problem. For example, statistics reveal that countries having economies that are freer tend to have a higher percentage of youth that dream of being entrepreneurs. A study shows that the United States of America, China, Japan, Singapore etc. have higher percentages of entrepreneurs among the population.[1]

The simple reason is that a restrictive economy removes the incentive for entrepreneurs, who are already undertaking huge risks even in the absence of restrictions from regulators. Thus, a practical way to remove lethargy would be the reduction in the roadblocks for entrepreneurs and reduce the risks for the youth as far as possible and not try to convert the youth into selfless Samaritans who would work all their life for Mizoram without personal ambitions. In the same way, since people

---

[1] Ratna Lindawati Lubis, *Assessing Entrepreneurial Leadership and the Law*: Why are these important for graduate students in Indonesia? (Indonesia: Telkom University, 2017)

who have accomplishments can walk with pride and develop healthy personalities, it would be much more effective to remove some of the moral restrictions placed on the youth by society and religions to reduce corruption and other dishonest trades.

The Mizo youth is also often blamed as being an indolent lot. They are scolded for not taking up the jobs that the non-Mizo people are taking, jobs such as cement work, brick laying, construction jobs etc. This is also a misplacing of priority.

If the Mizo youth do not take up low paying jobs, it is simply because they can afford not to.

Viewing this as a negative phenomenon is detrimental for the psychology of the Mizo youth. This is not to say that nothing should be done about the unemployed Mizo youth. The focus should be on discovering why unemployment occurs in the first place. The Mizo youth is pressured to attain high academic degrees. This inevitably causes underemployment, as it is strikingly evident that these graduates chase the same types of jobs due to their similar competencies. Hence, the root cause of the problem is that the society is unaware of the economics of the job market.

Another example of a misplaced priority would be the effort put in by the people, which is implemented through the government, for the improvement of education so as to produce the best bureaucrats and politicians who will form a good government, who will make Mizoram conquer the obstacles and lead it to a land of prosperity. It is easy to fall into this fallacy because there is a general belief that our education system is sub-par. This may be true to a certain extent. However, a look at how the rest of India is performing would show a different picture.

States such as Bihar and Uttar Pradesh have contributed the maximum number of candidates who have cleared UPSC, but the irony is that these states are not performing well in terms of development.

Since these supposed brightest brains have failed to achieve what we are currently dreaming of achieving, there is a clear misunderstanding of what our aim should be. Moreover, entities in India that have performed well tend to have some form of political insulation in one form or the other. Examples of these would be the Defence Research and Development Organisation, The Election Commission of India, The Indian Institute of Technology or the Indian Space Research Organisation. The Aizawl Municipal Corporation has also performed surprisingly well, and has held a firm stand on contentious issues. A common feature of these organisations is that they have some form of autonomy. These institutions do not always take in candidates from the highest level of competitions and are not manned by angelic creatures that are immune to corruption, but they have done very well, and have achieved impressive results. When the people vote, they have to select all of the manifestoes of the parties, which is akin to someone walking into a shop, and is forced to buy the whole shop. Since this is an inherent problem of a government which affects its effectiveness, it is important to see that those higher levels of competition during recruitment of the personnel, do not necessarily yield higher outputs.

The simple reason why entities that have autonomy perform better is that failure is more visible. This pushes the employees to continue learning on the job after the recruitment, unlike most government departments where the employees behave like they have hit the pinnacle of success once they are recruited. A department that is directly under the direct supervision of a minister has too many steps in the ladder of responsibility that it becomes almost impossible to blame a particular person. Moreover, the failure of the department hardly affects the job security of its employees, if the failure is detected at all. An autonomous institution has a smaller objective and a smaller group of people, both of which are very visible when things go wrong. The institution could even be dismantled if such failures persist. This is the same phenomenon that exists, and also at a much faster pace in the private sector. Economists call this 'creative destruction,' as new entities quickly fill up the void where the destruction had taken place. This misunderstanding was very visible when there were complaints regarding the recruitment of employees of the Mizoram Assembly Secretariat during the year 2023, or the suspicions which popped up in 2024 around how MPSC evaluates examination papers.

People were quick to point out that these alleged nepotisms were due to the autonomy enjoyed by these entities. However, they fail to see that the recruitment that looked like nepotism or unfairness for the public was visible precisely due to the fact that the entities had autonomy, as they had a relatively lesser number of people involved in it, and hence corrective actions had to be taken. It would be difficult to assume that nepotism has never occurred in other departments, as it is more believable that since these departments have a larger number of people involved, it becomes more difficult to detect the occurrences of such type of nepotism. The prescription from the people would be to set up some type of board, which invariably involves political leaders to oversee the recruitment. If such a board were set up, the people involved in the recruitment would increase exponentially, and the difficulty for the detection of nepotism would also increase exponentially. The members of the board would be appointed by a powerful politician, who has a number of people supporting him, while the members would also have their own priorities. Thus, it is important to see that solutions that are prescribed without a proper analysis often exacerbate the problems.

Wasteful Spending on Human Resources

Another misplaced priority that is visible from the executive side of the government that is common not just in Mizoram but throughout India is the focus to understand the technology and the means behind the production of goods for economic development. This is wrong in the sense that a government does not have the ability to run businesses, nor guide businessmen or the farmers, on how to improve their profit margins due to the simple reason that while the government recruits the best and the brightest to run its entities, it has almost always performed worse than the private sector. This is due to the simple reason that the job of a government is to govern, not to run businesses. Therefore, sending government servants or even political leaders to other states and abroad to study new technology is a waste of public money. Instead, the job of a government is to limit itself to signing trade treaties with other countries, remove hurdles for businesses, provide research funding for institutions or provide collaboration platforms, ensure safety for business logistics and speedily look into tax laws so as to not block business growth.

6

Fallacies Around Inequality

A common misconception among a large number of people, which is not limited to the people of Mizoram, is that if the economy were to be left on its own, the rich would swallow up all the assets and the poor people would be left with nothing. Moreover, there is a perception that if the income distribution is not closely monitored, the income equalities would increase due to the assumption of it being open ended. This argument appears to be logical, and does not appear the need for a closer study if one does not look at the evidence.

A quick glance of the minimum wages in Mizoram issued by the government during the past 20 years shows that wages of unskilled labour has been increasing at around 8% per year, which is well above the inflation rate in India. Wages have seen a substantial increase even among the unorganized services such as housemaids, where the wages have increased from around Rs. 3500 to Rs. 7000 within just a decade. Thus, saying that wages are decreasing or that the poor are getting poorer is simply untrue, as the purchasing power of people is increasing, even at the bottom.

What people often fail to see is that with the increase in standard of living, the needs of the people also tend to increase. We cannot compare our lives with that of the people who had to walk on foot. Dr. Sashi Tharoor had rightly said that the middle class today have a better breakfast than the kings of England back in the days. People in the past did not have to pay internet bills, electricity bills, medical bills, water bills, pay loans on houses made of modern materials and account for EMIs on scooter loans. We can look at these bills as burdens or privileges. If one chooses, switching back to the 'good old days' is simple; simply stop subscribing to these modern amenities. We always have the option to make our own salt, collect our own water from the river, travel on foot, light a fire for warmth, build houses with our own hands and grow our own crops. Thus, even if people cannot pay for all of these modern amenities and are only able to enjoy some of them, we are still better off than our ancestors.

We are living in a time where the food that we eat comes from all parts of the globe. This does not happen on its own; it requires a number of highly skilled people working around the clock to make it happen. Thus, if a certain section of people cannot enjoy all of the benefits of the modern system, that is not a total failure of the system. It only shows that the system has imperfections or that the results of development have not fully penetrated into some sections of the economy. Arriving to the conclusion that the current system is repressive and that the poor are getting poorer and the rich are getting richer is simply untrue, dangerous and can be a breeding ground for radicalism. This type of thinking has a very high tendency to lead people to the dangerous ideals of communism. Moreover, even if the current system fails to deliver, it is not evident that the old system was better, as there was not much of a system in the past to begin with. People were mostly left to fend for themselves, which is incomparable to the current system that we have today. 'Rosy retrospection' is a cognitive bias with which people tend to remember the past better than it actually was, and we must be careful not to fall prey to it while discussing economics.

Wealth Redistribution

There is another argument which says that the wealth that is generated is not equally shared, and thus this needs to be fixed. The first part which says that there is inequality is true, and does not require much debate. However, the argument that this needs fixing and the measures that are suggested are often illogical, and sometimes downright dangerous. It is of course undesirable that with the global GDP continuously increasing, many people are still living in poverty. It is also not wrong to accept the notion that the wealth generated has not trickled down enough. But, suggesting that the wealth should be taken directly from the rich and given to the people at the bottom can be very dangerous. First of all, who would be taking the wealth and giving it to the poor? 'Yes, it's the government, the government is the best agent to do it.' The people should select the best to handle this transfer, and everyone would be happy. Right? Well, there are some questions to ask. First, where has this ever worked on a large scale? What has happened is that the people who promised to transfer wealth equally, end up having all the riches and power, while the people remain poor. Secondly, is it economically sustainable? Can we really take wealth and transfer it at a large scale? The Microsoft Company has its wealth in the form of shares that are held by millions of people. Should Mr. Bill Gates not sell his shares and give them to other people? Well, he could definitely do that. But there is another way. He could keep the dividends and reinvest into his company, which further grows his business and creates more job opportunities. So, either way, other people benefit from the process. Moreover, even if he spends the money from his company, his money would still go to other businesses, who also have employees. So, to say that wealth creation does not benefit the poor and that the people at the top keep all the money is simply untrue. We also have to accept the reality that some people are not qualified to hold a lot of wealth, and the people who create wealth are invaluable as they give the wealth its value. A 20-year study conducted by wealth consultancy, The Williams Group, involved over 3,200 families and found that seven in ten families tend to lose their fortune by the second generation, while nine in ten lose it by the third generation. This shows that 'the rich' are also not a particular group of people. Whom we call rich is continuously changing and people move in and out of this assigned 'rich' category.

Fictional Wealth

There is also a general misunderstanding of how fictional wealth operates. Most of the fictional wealth that has been created is based on the notion that these entities will continue to generate wealth for a long time. For example, a quick calculation shows that most of the companies in India that generate a stable profit are valued around ten times their annual earnings, after adjusting for the time value of money. This means that the fictional wealth of the shareholders is based on the belief that the people working in these companies will eventually repay them by growing these companies. So, the faith of the shareholders in the promoters of these companies is what props-up the value of the companies. The assumption that one can simply take the valuations of these companies and transfer it to the people who need it more, would simply erode all the wealth, which is exactly what happened when Hugo Chavez, the then President of Venezuela went around his country and ordered private properties to be expropriated. In places where people are free, there is simply no need to transfer the wealth from the current holders to someone else. The focus must be on how to create more wealth, increase social mobility and increase freedom.

It is also important to understand the forces at play which lead to inequality. People often have the perception that inequality is caused by the design or the will of some particular people, while it is more of an emergent property that arises as a result of the cumulative decisions of all the people taking part in an economy.

A rich person cannot be blamed for buying a Lamborghini, even though the owner is already rich in the same way that a poor woman who buys a cheap meal from a McDonald's is doing nothing wrong, even though the CEO earns crores of rupees every year. Our decisions are based on the most economical or the most pleasing option at that moment.

The teammates of Lionel Messi cannot be blamed for passing the ball to him when he had already scored 60 goals during that year. They are passing the ball to him simply because it is good for the team.

When it comes to the economy, large entities such as the government or corporations are blamed when they allot their capital that benefits the rich people. The fact is that even poor people are doing the same thing. The only difference is that the people with less wealth are doing it at a smaller scale, and hence it is less visible. It is simply illogical to buy things from a person just because he is poor. People only do this out of charity, and it never forms a big part of their spending. While India was reeling under tension from China along its border, the so-called patriotic citizens continued to purchase Chinese electronic items.

Although this action was condemned, their behaviour is completely normal and is actually good for the country, as an increase in the volume of trade tends to decrease conflicts among countries, and it makes it inconvenient for political leaders to continue aggressive tactics.

Debunking the Arguments Against Growth

There is a certain section of people in Mizoram who argue that we should not only aim for growth, but try to prevent the growth from going out of control. This argument, like other arguments for economic control, is well-intentioned. They argue that growth should not come at the cost of the poor sections of the society. This is a misunderstanding of economics to the extreme. Looking at data for living standards, immigration and freedom of the people, growth is a strong factor. Growth has allowed people to come out of poverty and has granted them the freedom to pursue their passion. Most people tend to have the wrong perception that poverty is something new, and is a creation of a wrong system. The truth is that poverty, just like slavery, has always been there, and is only visible recently in human history as growth and development has rendered them visible. The people are only recently granted the opportunity to be discontented about their living conditions. Complaining about the very thing that granted people the freedom to dream looks tempting at times, but it is an extremely dangerous endeavour.

What people call capitalism is nothing but the culmination of choices of the people. These very same people often claim that someone else is responsible, which is exceptionally hypocritical. The people who claim that corporations are evil and that their entry into Mizoram would destroy the state, would happily buy their products because they are cheap. Buying the best option available is nothing out of the ordinary and we simply have to start being honest about it. People tend to choose based on the utility, not the love for their country or their economic ideals. A diversion from this natural phenomenon would surely backfire, as is evident in many countries across the globe. Suppression of human desires and blocking the people's freedom to follow their passion is a sure way to an economic down-spiral. Imposing socialist ideals on the people is very limiting, which forces people to look for other outlets to fulfil their ambitions, which is usually outside the ambit of the law. To check those illegal behaviors, governments tend to impose more control, thus leading to a downward spiral of people's freedom along with the economy.

The assumption that people who are not under regulation will not take care of each other discounts an important factor, which is that humans have empathy.

Except for the few people who lack the ability to empathize due to medical reasons, everyone has this ability. This is a crucial factor for the development of modern society, as people who were emphatic were more productive for their units when humans were living as tribes. Thus, the belief that people who are left to themselves would end up in a downward spiral is not only wrong, but also dangerous.

The reader should now be able to decipher that the aim should be neither a bottom up nor a top bottom, but a market-oriented economy. The reason why socialist and communist economies fail is not because the welfare measures are inherently bad, but rather due to the restrictions placed upon the fire of human desire to grow. These types of economies require a planner, and the planner can only know so much. Moreover, even the perfect plan would be wrong for at least a significant portion of the population due to the simple reason that people's goals, ambitions and capabilities are different. Hence, debating the ills of capitalism or that of socialism is futile. The only point of debate should be whether a government should intervene in a particular subject, and if so, to what extent, always bearing in mind the natural behavior of a government and the people in general.

7

A Belief that Government is the Economy

Economic discussions among the people of Mizoram are mainly focused on the government and its activities. Some even go further to say that tax losses due to illegal smuggling is a loss not just for the government, but for the people. This assumption of loss has become particularly visible after the illegal trade of areca-nut from Myanmar that grew in volume. In a country where the government has its hand on almost all aspects of economic activities, it is an appealing assumption, but nevertheless wrong.

It is certainly true that a government is the largest single entity in the economic ecosystem. However, there are other players which form a part of the economy. Saying that a person who does not pay tax causes an economic loss to the state neglects all other players of the economy. The important thing to look at in this situation is the 'trade-off' i.e. how does the spending of the person or the firm compare to the spending quality of the government.

The uncomfortable truth is that government spending usually causes a net loss because of its inherent nature, which is its inefficiency. Therefore, a person who evades tax cannot be pre-assumed to cause an economic loss to the state, even if that person does not have the habit of maximizing the output from his spending. Many people also forget that as a government is incapable of running a business as it tends to run into losses, the resources of the government are obtained from private businesses. In the case of Mizoram, huge devolutions and schemes from the central government make it appear that the government has the ability to actually create wealth. While writing this book, the tax contribution to the central government kitty is about 0.1%, while the receipt is about 0.5% of the total devolution. This gives legitimacy to the government to do almost anything to the economy, and also allows the people to live in seclusion from the other states, which would otherwise be unsustainable economically. The people look to the government to bring business, but regard private investment as harmful. They disregard the economic booms around the world brought by private equity, and continue to stress on the importance of spending government funds correctly. A large number of people also argue that the government should consider imposing more tax. They also misunderstand that the income tax waiver which is granted to the people of Northeast India should be removed so as to allow the government to spend more, while income tax is exclusively under the union list.

The people of Mizoram who discuss the economy also mainly talk of the government. The press in Mizoram also rarely focuses on businesses. Rather, they focus on government meetings, project inaugurations and government scheme implementations. Business news rarely occupies the front page. They also would point out the flaws of the government and its bureaucrats as they strongly believe that an efficient government equates to a good economy. When talking about jobs in the private sector, the norm is that other jobs are discussed as an addition to government jobs. They do not highlight that the main driver of the economy should be the private sector, as it is the sector that is actually capable of creating wealth. Even if the current situation in Mizoram is opposite to the natural order due to artificial regulations, it does not change the natural order itself.

8

The Strong Government Fallacy

Some statements are totally fallacious, while some are true to a certain extent. However, it is important to point out the extent of the truth as the impact of a half-truth can be equally devastating. It will be even more difficult to correct the fallacy in the case of a statement that contains elements of truth in it since it becomes very tedious to decipher the right elements from the wrong contents. It would require a highly specialised professional to point out where the exact problems are hidden among the well-intentioned programs and regulations of the government.

Luckily, there are ways of solving this infinitely complex problem. Economists have found ways to come to reasonable conclusions by looking at empirical data from various countries. A look at various data shows that a strong government can be a driver of growth, but it can also be the reason for the stagnation of the economy at the same time. Strength in terms of providing physical security can play a vital role in improving the economy of a country, but providing a financial safety net has almost always backfired.

While it is tempting to provide more and more welfare to citizens, it requires an increase in the role of the government on the economy. This stronger government requires money, which it happily collects from the people. Moreover, the intervention of the government has a 'crowding out' effect on private businesses. This effect is not immediate and does not affect all people at once, which is why people tend to quickly disregard it. On the other hand, the positive effects of the new government intervention can be immediately seen, and even to those people that are not beneficiaries to it, there are not many reasons for negative feelings about these interventions. In a way, it is a lot like excessive deficit spending, which brings a euphoria at the beginning, but causes painful inflation in the long run. The ill-effects of a constrained economy are felt slowly but surely in the long run, and it is often very difficult to remove the intervention as removing it would cause an immediate harm to its beneficiaries, while the positive effects take time to be felt by the people.

For example, outsiders are mostly not allowed to run their businesses in Mizoram. This is implemented by the people through the government because they feel that outsiders will outcompete them, causing a loss of livelihood for Mizo people. This belief is partly true, but it neglects the ill-effects. The positive effects are immediately felt by the people as there are more opportunities for Mizo businessmen with little competition. But the long term ill-effect is that the low competition results in high prices, lack of business connection with other states leading to smaller markets for Mizo traders, constraints on the influx of private investments and sub-par customer service for the people. These ill-effects appear to have no connection to the ban of outsiders for someone who does not pay close attention. Therefore, people blame these ill-effects on other factors such as the greed of the Mizo people, the lack of business skills among the Mizos or the lack of political will in the government. They view the positive effects as separate phenomena from the ill-effects. Thus, there is no effort to address the root cause of the problem. Instead, they seek more government intervention to remove these ill-effects, such as price controls, filing of complaints in consumer courts and an increased government vigilance over these businesses. When the people see that these ill-effects are not solved, they continue to blame the government. Little do they know that giving a permit to the government to tightly regulate businesses is a risky endeavor. Tight regulation on businesses draws people away from the profession, as it increases business risk, causing the best minds to choose other professions. This artificial lack of talent in the business profession further exacerbates the problem.

Regulation

There is another misconception that regulation is good for the economy. Ideally, regulation should be allowed only to the extent that the regulation provides a level playing field for the businesses. People tend to believe that businesses of different places have a different effect on the economy. Due to this, governments around the world have placed taxes on goods and services under fancy names such as anti-dumping duty, cess, import duty and the likes. While most economists and multilateral agencies such as the World Trade Organizations, World Bank etc. know full well that open trade mutually benefits both trading partners, the general belief of the people, which is reflected in the politics of a country or a state, controls the decision-making process.

Economist Milton Friedman went as far as to say that even if a country has no exports, it still benefits from the imports alone, thus refuting the idea that trade deficits are bad for a country or a state.

In fact, Mizoram would prove to be a very strong evidence for his point. If Mizoram were to sustain itself with only the goods and services that it produces, it would abruptly revert back to the stone age. A state that does not mine minerals and does not have the skilled labour or the entities to manufacture the simplest of machines is in the worst position to argue for restrictions on businesses and their products from other states, but a large number of people in Mizoram are ironically doing exactly that. The people from a state that exports next to nothing, and are benefitting from the innovation and entrepreneurial skills of people from other states are currently afraid that opening up further will hurt them. Meanwhile, they continue to rely on the efforts of the people that have taken the pain to produce these technologies.

They believe that if only the government could help the poor and does not engage in corruption, then their problems would go away, while the uncomfortable truth is that they are the people who are actually guiding the government to move in the wrong direction.

Countries going for de-regulation and adopting market-oriented approaches tend to do better. This point was stated by the World Bank in the case of Vietnam on its recent above par performance.[2] The presence of a big percent of the population of Mizoram who feel that the government should regulate away their problems and eliminate poverty is a hurdle that does not appear to be going away in the near future. Whenever these people see

---

[2] John R. Dodsworth et al, *Vietnam Transition to a Market Economy* (Washington DC: IMF, 1996)

a problem, they urge the government to step in. And when the government does step in, people who are not engaged in the actual business do the planning. Since these bureaucrats do not actually experience the problems, the solution that they provide turns out to be inefficient.

Moreover, the government servants do not pay the price for being wrong, as proper research into the effects of government interventions are rarely conducted. Furthermore, the more the problems that are perceived by the people that needs government intervention, the more avenues that open up for exercising influence and control by the politicians and the bureaucrats. Hence, there is a very little push to reduce the sphere of influence of the government, except for the feeble voices from a few people who try to argue that people have to take responsibility for their own life and not remain too dependent on the government.

9

Fallacies Around Inflation

The simple inflation adjusted calculation of increase in prices does not show the actual picture in many instances. Improvements in living standards as well as technology have added many new features to our homes, cars, phones and tools. These features are often overlooked when calculating inflation in an economy. Features such as air conditioners, soundproofing, safety systems, seat belts, brake assist systems, more comfortable seats and a better fuel mileage due to onboard computer systems are now available as standard in most cars today. A simple comparison of the prices of cars today with those of the past overlooks these improvements. These features do not come for free. They require innovation, labour and materials. A correct calculation must include these changes so as to account for the new costs that have been included for manufacturing these cars.

In the same way, houses have also improved. In a modern house, the cost of construction has increased due to improvements in building materials as well as the inclusion of new facilities that were previously unavailable. For example, houses were mostly made of wood or mud along with stones in the olden days. Today, houses are made of concrete. The production of cement is a complex process that has been discovered recently. If we were to build a house the way it was done in the past, the prices would not be as high as today. Houses have also come with sophisticated paints, modern electrification, with a lot more lights, floors that are plastered, bathrooms that come with modern faucets along with running water, sophisticated sinks and even bathtubs. All these changes are overlooked by the people who think that houses are increasing in price and have left the poor behind, while it is a fact that even the poor are improving in their housing in most countries.

There is also a common misconception among the Mizo people wherein they attribute the things which they regard as sinful or unfair such as corruption, smuggling or greed as factors for inflation. However, arguments from the viewpoint of either a Monetarist or a Modern Monetary Theorist, or even an Austrian economist would not directly attribute the cause for inflation to these factors. Corruption would not cause an increase in money supply if it does not have the ability to disseminate more money than the normal legal norm established by law. A greedy person does not have the ability to arbitrarily increase prices if the customer is unwilling to pay for it. And a smuggler would hardly be able to increase the money supply in Mizoram to make a dent in the GSDP. The people refuse to look at the truth that is staring right at them, which is that government schemes disburse a huge quantity of money to the market. Since government activities are based on the Keynesian method of creating demand, it is forever prone to the supply demand mismatch due to central planning. Thus, the money that is disbursed to the market often does not continue to find products to buy, resulting in more money chasing the same number of goods, and thus causing inflation.

Land Price Inflation

The conflation of equality with that of inflation by comparing the status of the rich with the poor to assess the cost of housing for the lower classes of society is also fallacious. The increase in prices of land has also been pointed out as a symptom of the evils of capitalism.

A comparison of the average cost of land today with that of the past overlooks the simple fact that land has become more valuable due to human ingenuity.

A small plot of land can now sustain businesses that earn a livelihood for a family. In the past, land was either used for agriculture or for building a house as commerce was limited.

Even today, land still has a very little value in some places in Mizoram. The village councils are freely allotting land to the people. Pointing to the prices of land in the city and saying that the price of land has skyrocketed without looking at the increased ability of the land to generate an income for its owner is wrong as it overlooks the other side of the coin. In fact, the Economic Survey of Mizoram also shows inflation to be higher in rural areas, which contradicts the claim that prices are skyrocketing in the towns.

Under normal circumstances, prices can increase only so far as the return matches the cost paid by the buyer, no matter how rich the buyer is. Of course, this overlooks speculators. However, speculators also buy into their positions, only with the belief that the asset could increase in price. The only catch is that speculators often make mistakes and pay an amount that is actually higher than the value. However, the speculators invariably realise the actual cost sooner or later.

Another fallacy that is often visible during the assessment of the rise in land value is the exclusion of value unlocking. Value unlocking occurs due to an increased settlement in a particular area, which could be due to government project, an investment by a private entity, and the general liking of the neighborhood by the people. The increased settlement of the people in that area tends to increase the land prices considerably. This increase in prices has often been regarded by the people as an increase in the general prices of the land. However, when a certain locality experiences an increase in prices of land due to an increased economic activity, it should not be regarded as inflation, but should be regarded as an unlocking in value. What is happening in this area is that the value of the land which was almost non-existent prior to the increased settlement in that area has now become almost at par with other areas of similar economic activities. Therefore, this must be kept in mind while calculating the increase in prices of the land. If this value unlocking is discounted during the calculation, it will show a very drastic inflation which seems to be problematic and will cause the people to blame capitalism, the ruling elites or sometimes the government. This phenomenon has been visible in the suburbs of Aizawl and recently in Champhai where economic activities have increased due to growing trade with the neighbouring country Myanmar.

Thus, viewing the increase in prices itself as a negative phenomenon and trying to control the increase in prices is going to create a lot of hurdles for investors, businessmen and home builders. Moreover, people also conveniently leave out the fact that the land owners who are now able to sell their land at higher prices are highly benefitted, as the anointed class is rarely focused on benefits but mostly on problems that need fixing. Seeing something that is positive as a negative phenomenon is a dangerous misconception which can lead to a stagnation of growth.

10

The Illusion of Price Control

Price control is not new. Price control gained the attention of economists during the Second World War. It is a tempting fruit for politicians. After all, who would want to take sides with the greedy businessmen! Take away some of the profits by putting a cap on the prices and you can control greed. It is a marvelous idea, but fallacious. It does not take very long for an economy to reveal that it is impossible to determine the so-called 'fair price' of the commodity or service. This is why 'fair price shops' have mostly become redundant in India.

Despite historical evidence, its contradiction with the law of supply and demand and its apparent failure within Mizoram itself, people are still convinced that there is an apparent need of an outside agency to control prices. The failure has become so embarrassingly evident that butchers are openly selling 800 grams of pork as a kilogram due to price control. Yet, people are still convinced that the greed of the butchers needs to be contained or else they would inflate prices to arbitrarily high levels.

The concept of price control fails to consider that prices are determined by market forces. It is an equilibrium point of the various forces at play. While it is challenging enough to determine an equilibrium point of a particular commodity of a particular place at a particular time among a particular set of players, it is highly unlikely that a single person or agency can correctly predict the correct prices of several items of various locations of constantly fluctuating players which is to take place at a future time, which is affected by a number of variables that cannot be predicted in advance such as calamities, increase or decrease in supply and the sentiments of players in the market.

Although not quite intrusive as the traditional price control, the Maximum Retail Price system, a favourite of the social justice warriors, also continues to be a major impediment for small businesses especially in remote areas of Mizoram. These MRPs are usually set by corporations considering the situations in the bigger cities. These prices are usually not sustainable for small businesses due to a number of factors such as cost of living, inability to take advantage of economies of scale, distance from cities etc. Although easily changeable, the printing of a price on a commodity puts the customer at a supposedly higher moral ground when the shopkeeper sells above that printed price. However, when the MRP does not reflect the actual input cost of that particular seller, the supposed higher moral ground does not have a leg to stand on. This false price restricts the growth of businesses in villages, which in turn allows only bigger businesses to operate, and is therefore anti-poor. Another phenomenon that often occurs under the MRP system is that businesses completely disregard the MRPs in places where the prices are impractical, which puts a moral baggage on the businesses. This moral baggage in variably lowers the desirability of the profession, which in turn leads to lesser number of businesses, which further leads to lesser competition, which ironically, leads to higher prices.

Higher prices could easily be lowered using the proven principles of economics instead by using methods that are not in accordance with these proven laws. The act of putting more restrictions is bound to create higher prices, even if that restriction is to put a price cap on commodities. The imbalance eventually seeps out in one form or the other. The black market is one such example. It is easy to put the blame on smugglers. After all, they are criminals. However, as you are inserting the key into the locks of the prison cells of these vicious criminals, it is important to recognize that the black market is the universe twisting your arm back for the imbalance that you have caused. This fallacy was clearly visible during the initial stage of implementing the new Goods and Services Tax system. The Central Government had tried to prevent what it called profiteering, as it believed that businessmen were profiting from the new tax regime. It was a complete disregard of the market forces, which was controlling the prices in the first place. A crackdown on the greed of businesses was unnecessary as any new room for profit that was available would be quickly discovered by other businesses, and would be instantly swallowed up by the market forces. Moreover, since the old marked prices on commodities were arbitrary, an effort to bring them to a correct new level does not make much sense. If it was mainly a political move to assuage fear, it could be forgiven. However, if the move was due to the fear that businesses would charge extra costs from customers, it did not make much sense.

I will try to explain why price control harms the economy by utilizing the bold claim that 'no one knows how to make a pencil,' an example given by economist Milton Friedman in one of his lectures. He explained that there is not one single person who knows how to make something as simple as a pencil, if he were to do it all by himself.

"The wood used in the pencil is grown in some part of the United States, which requires felling by an expert. The graphite may be mined in some part of another country, while the eraser on the top may be made of rubber, which may be grown in Indonesia or even India. The paint to cover the wood is made in some factory, which contains several additives. The metal which houses the eraser is also mined in some country which may be outside the United States. Even after all the parts are available, it still requires a pencil factory, a factory which requires several different areas of expertise such as lawyers who will undertake the legal requirements, engineers who know how to build and maintain the machines that help in the assembling of the pencil, salespersons who will sell the product, and managers who will take care of the employees".

All these things are required to make something as simple as a pencil, which is possible only through the magic of the free price system. Many of the people who are involved in the making of the pencil are not from the same country, and do not even speak the same language. Yet, they coordinate even without realizing. They coordinate only due to the incentive behind each of their actions. This is quickly taken away when the freedom of price is taken away from them. Hence, it is not wise to impose price controls on any type of commodity, even for the so-called essential commodities. All commodities are essential to the person who needs it. A better way to ensure the availability of basic necessities such as food, water or electricity is diversification, and not price control. Even during times of crisis, price control should only be used as a temporary measure, as it requires a very large amount of government control to actually implement it.

For example, when people were informed that curfews were going to be imposed during covid, people started piling up on essential kitchen items. Luckily, normalcy was quickly reattained as people could quickly receive information via the internet. If this would have happened before good internet connectivity, the problem would have been many magnitudes worse. If prices were allowed to fluctuate freely, the hoarding of these commodities would be controlled by the increase in prices, caused by the increase in demand. The people who could not afford the temporary high prices could easily be helped by the government by giving cash directly to them, and also by charitable organizations. When the items are gone, it is almost impossible even for the government to help the people in need of essential supplies. The only way would be to place law enforcement personnel out on the streets every day for 24 hours, which would breed other problems such as corruption among the law enforcement officials. It would also quickly create black markets. Thus, the traits of a totalitarian government would quickly be donned by the government. Many of the less serious situations such as price rise due to false information of scarcity can be easily tackled by providing the correct information swiftly and effectively by the government's departments that handle public relations, through which embarrassing situations like the hoarding of the common salt by the Mizo people can be avoided.

It is noticeable that prices of most commodities are costlier in the north-eastern states of Mizoram. Discussions by the people of Mizoram on high prices often tend to overlook this similar problem that is also occurring right outside our doorstep. Instead, blame is placed on politicians, businessmen and also almost everyone, everyone except the one who is professing the need for price control. It is quite evident that prices in Mizoram and also the other north-eastern states are going to be higher when compared to the plains due to economics such as size of market, distance required for transportation, risk for truckers due to government restrictions for outsiders, illegal collection of money by some NGOs and poor quality of roads. The government may be able to fix the quality of the road, but the other hurdles cannot be removed by the government without public support. Public support does not appear to be coming anytime soon, as assimilation alarmists are trying their best to maintain the purity of the Mizo race. These alarmists do not realize that they are creating the economics for high prices in Mizoram, and they are often the very same people who place blame on everyone but themselves for the high prices. They also often urge the government to implement price control measures, not realizing that governments can only control prices, but not the costs.

When the prices mandated by law are not sustainable, the market tends to resort to unlawful practices such as black markets. This black market is again blamed on the lack of integrity and the lack of the true Christian faith among Mizo people. We must however, accept that prices will have a propensity to be higher in Mizoram than most of the other states in India due to the geographical location of the state. Focus must be placed on how to sustain the economy despite the higher prices, instead of trying to achieve the impossible task of removing it. The aim must be to improve the income of the people so as to be able to afford the higher prices and also achieve economies of scale to keep it at healthy levels.

It is also pertinent to understand that different places have different prices. Higher prices do not automatically equal harsher living conditions. On the contrary, people often move to places having higher prices due to the availability of more economic opportunities in these places.

Tenancy Rates

It is easy to say that rent is too high, and the landlords are greedy, supplemented by the assertion that the rich are getting richer and they are taking advantage of the poor. This notion has led people to believe that the prices of rent in the city are exploitative and therefore, need to be controlled. However, they fail to see that the landlord is only acting under the force of the market, among which is the rent that is being paid by the tenant. Landlords cannot impose what they like, due to the simple fact that they also have other landlords to compete with and the tenant is free to choose from among the list of empty homes available for rent. Rent in Aizawl and the more populated district capitals such as Lunglei, Champhai, Kolasib et cetera can be divided into two categories, namely

A. Houses that are rented to families and

B. Houses that are rented to businesses.

The rent that is paid by families is not at par with the rent that is paid by business establishments. A quick calculation will show that the rent that is paid by families is not a very good investment for the homeowner, and are, therefore usually the basement or the ground floors or some vacant portions of the houses that are built by the home owners who are using it to live in them themselves. On the other hand, commercial buildings do exist and the rates are much higher and are viable investments for the owners. Private hostels have also increased in number and are proving to be viable investments for the owners, and fall under the commercial category. The people who claim that the rates are too high usually think about families and is therefore of the lower rent category. Thus, it is quite evident that the claim made by the people regarding rent is without evidence and is merely an emotional response to the complaints of tenants. What tends to happen among the Mizo community, and also among many other communities is that when a complaint is raised by a weaker section of the society, they take it without looking at the evidence and pass it on as something infallible. This is fuelled by the cognitive ease that is provided by other social problems that they are already familiar with. The actual solution, if there was actually a problem, would be to try to make it easier for home builders to build more houses, lower taxes so as to decrease the cost of construction materials, improve transportation, adopt innovative methods of building houses to lower costs, make land easily accessible to home builders etc. and to also try to improve the economic conditions of the people by boosting the economy.

11

The Sustainable Economy Fallacy

After the emergence of the climate change crisis, and along with it, the sustainability of the economy, people often conflate environmental sustainability with economic sustainability. I call this the 'sustainable economy fallacy'. People are worried about what would happen if the present trend continues on the exploitation of natural resources. However, very little thought is spared for the sustainability of our economic activities in Mizoram. We have a propensity to believe that projects are successful when they are completed, even after the government itself has demanded an outcome analysis on its projects. Businesses that are environmentally sustainable are also simply assumed to be sustainable economically. The people also like to point out that development must happen equally in the cities and the villages without crunching the numbers. Without actual calculations, they fail to see the exorbitantly high cost of developing villages that are located in remote places with very little population. Each village requires a road, an electricity grid, water supply, doctors, nurses, hospitals, teachers, and internet connections. When people assume that a government providing these facilities is doing good for the economy, they are ignoring the fact that the money required to provide these services was forcefully taken by the government from other people. Even if these facilities do develop the villages, the result can still be a net loss for the economy. Thus, we must not hesitate to treat these provisions as charity instead of automatically assuming that they are contributing to development, except when a potential for realistic economic viability is available in the long term. Hence, focus should be placed on identifying the potential for self-sustaining businesses with the help of researchers for each village, instead of applying common schemes for all the villages. Micro analysis is a must, especially for villages in Mizoram with features that are vastly different from other Indian villages.

12

The Greedy Banker Fallacy

The banking system is a mysterious entity for the common man. This mystery around banks, which appears to be a worldwide phenomenon, has aroused much suspicion. Mizoram is not an exception. Bankers are regarded as greedy businessmen who only operate their banks for the sake of profit. This fallacy stems directly from the misunderstanding of profit, which will also be discussed in detail. The people's sentiments are directly reflected in the policies of the government and the Reserve Bank of India, which try to regulate the capital allocation of banks using various methods. Bankers are often blamed for not allocating resources to the poorer sections of the society. Various committees are set up by the government to oversee the performances of the banks so as to ensure that resources are allocated in the supposed 'correct manner'. After all, why would the greedy bankers help the poor when their only objective is to make the maximum profit.

The central government has also devised schemes to be funded by loans from banks. The burden to fund these schemes is placed not just on government owned banks, but also on private banks. This strategy is a clever method of the government to escape the debt ceiling enacted by law.

The control placed upon bankers should, in theory, help the citizens and bring people out of poverty. However, the evidence does not seem to support this. We often fail to see that many people are stuck in poverty due to the simple fact that they are in professions that are outdated, non-profitable or are out-competed in their trade. The most common allocation from these government mandated loans is usually on these professions that are no longer viable or unprofitable; such an example would be traditional agriculture. Government officials also tend to blame the banks for achieving low credit to deposit ratios, while forgetting the fact that the job of the banker, or the economy for that matter is to allocate its resources where it achieves the best return, be it in terms of interest rate or risk. Thus, the focus should be on improving the credit risk of the people, rather than urging the bankers to allocate more resources to Mizoram. If the bankers find good opportunities, they will organically invest in Mizoram without much need for compulsion.

Data released by the Reserve Bank of India shows government owned banks are performing much worse and are destroyers of wealth for their investors. The private banks on average grow at a much higher pace, compound the wealth of their investors and create more job opportunities. This contradicts the claim that the greedy bankers need to be controlled as the banks that are better controlled are the government owned banks. The banks that are doing what appears to be ethically correct are creating less wealth, job opportunities or growth. Rather, they require bail out packages from the government which are funded by taxpayer money in contrast to private banks, who usually pay the price for allocating their funds incorrectly.

The fallacy around the working of banks prevents the people from being financially literate. The reluctance to learn more about banks also cause the people develop unhealthy relationships with the banking industry. Parents do not teach their children to try to have a healthy bank transaction history as soon as possible. Minimum balances mandated by banks are also treated as anti-poor, forgetting the fact that it is necessary for maintaining the liquidity of the banks.

13

The Inner Line Permit Fallacy

The Inner Line Permit system was installed to protect the vulnerable smaller groups of people in the north-eastern part of India. This ILP restricts the influx of non-tribals from other areas into the region. This constitutional provision holds a special place in the hearts of the people living within these areas. It is often seen as the only protection against assimilation. This movement restriction also goes in line with the reservation system where people of a particular group are granted special rights for enrolment into institutions and hiring for government jobs. This much cherished legal provision is often misconstrued as a boon to the economy and the society. This could be nothing further from the truth. Empirical evidence has shown that countries that are segregated in terms of trade have always fared worse compared to countries that are open.

The biggest economic hindrance due to the implementation of the inner line permit system is that while it blocks the flow of investments from wealthy industrialists and talented individuals into the state, there is still an influx of economically backward people as these poorer people are the ones who are willing to take the risk of being prosecuted and face the various discriminations imposed on non-locals. Thus, the net result is that while the restriction is very successful in blocking the influx of investments and highly skilled individuals into the state, it has failed to block unskilled and semi-skilled workers, who are often looked at with disdain and this is regarded as a symptom of corruption and hypocrisy of the politicians and the individuals who are involved in helping the movement of these workers into the state. The benefit that we receive from the influx of low skilled workers is the lowering of the wage rate, thus lowering prices to a certain extent. However, large investments from outsiders are mostly non-existent.

People will quickly point out that a lack of investors in Mizoram is due to lack of opportunities. This argument quickly crumbles when we look at the investments in the Middle East, which is mostly desert. The investment started when investors started feeling they were welcomed into these countries and tax benefits were provided. The how and why of investment was decided by the investors, and not the government or the citizens of these countries. Thus, it would be wise to not try to find out what the opportunities are, and instead focus on opening up the Mizoram economy, and the investors will do the thinking for themselves.

While we make the argument of opening the economy, it must be said that there are benefits attached to having a homogeneous society. A homogeneous society provides the luxury of having a close-knit society who are emphatic towards one another, which helps to control poverty and inequality. However, we have been overlooking the downside. This neglect has led people to not look for opportunities without compromising too much on the advantages. The goal must be to bring in the best of both worlds.

There has also been a certain level of hypocrisy among the activists when it comes to keeping non-local businesses out of Mizoram. While brands like such as Louis Phillipe, West Side, KFC etc. which are perceived to possess a certain level of respect do not seem to receive much resistance, smaller businesses and brands face a lot of hostility. Amazon has also penetrated Mizoram market successfully. This shows that many of the decisions made by the people are emotional, and not strategic.

A common fallacy when people analyze business competition is that they give local businesses and businesses of non-locals different importance, while the economy sees absolutely no difference between them. For the economy, and ultimately the consumer, a greater number of businesses are always better as it creates more competition. The people tend to see only the negative effects of the shift in employment and growth, while conveniently leaving out the positive effects out in their analysis. This type of one-sided reasoning is dangerous and has been a perennial roadblock for economic growth. People also use a similar type of reasoning when new technological innovations which render some jobs obsolete come to the market. They say that these innovations will drive poor people out of their jobs and create more unemployment, while the truth is staring right at them. Any state in a country like India that had seen the magic of economic liberalization in the 1990s should not need another lesson on the importance of opening up the economy, but we still have a large number of people who still choose to follow the pre 1990 economic model.

14

Fallacies Around a Planned Economy

There is a general perception among people that more planning equates more growth. This is a logical conclusion considering that the rate of success is higher at an individual level when the actions are pre-planned. So, by extension, it is only logical that a planned economy would be better than an unplanned economy. Thus, it is not surprising that a Planning Commission was established in India. This mighty institution would plan the economy of India and drive growth towards the best possible outcome. The Planning Commission was dismantled and was replaced by Niti Aayog. However, the policies under the new system are still heavily laced with the concept of planning instead of a market- oriented approach. Mizoram also still has a Planning Department and still performs more or less the same functions.

Much to the dismay of the social justice warriors, planning is harmful for the economy. This is due to the simple reason that it is impossible to predict where the next Tesla or Microsoft is going to come from. The shoots of growth tend to look ugly at the beginning, and we tend to regulate it out of the economy. Countries that have tried to plan their economy tend to see a mismatch between supply and demand. It is troubling to see that so many people in Mizoram want the government to plan the economy and lift them out of their current situation. This mindset itself is already a side-effect of a paternalistic government where the people want someone else to do their bidding for them, and also blame someone else for their failures.

Planning requires control, and this control which leads to over-regulation by the government and by the society itself blocks the incentives to innovate and to start a successful enterprise. Technological innovation and risky enterprises, which are the backbone to grow an economy in the long term, tend to look grotesque at the beginning. There may be a need to develop tolerance towards these tender shoots of growth. These different enterprises that do not fit inside the economic plan could provide the diversification that is needed to reduce the dependency on the government.

Bringing Opportunity Cost into the Equation

The Government of India devises schemes out of the tax that is collected by both the central government states and the union territories. These are broadly classified into Centrally Sponsored Schemes and Central Schemes. Additionally, there are also other grants and loans in various forms, which have more or less the same purpose, all aimed at harmonizing the growth of the country in a direction that is aligned with the policies of the ruling party. This is an age-old practice in India, and is a feature in many other countries as well. These well-intentioned schemes do have many advantages, as there are common challenges for the states in India. We could argue that the public goods such as roads, internet connectivity, or electricity are suitable for public spending but other types of spending, although well intentioned, tend to produce more problems than they solve.

Losses are usually reported when the money spent on a project is seen as ineffective. A building that is not commissioned and is in ruins or a water supply that is unable to pump come to mind. This is a correct analysis and does not require further deliberation. However, these analyses often leave out the concept of opportunity cost. To completely bring out the gains and losses for any government development activity, the analysis must start from the collection of the taxes, and the utilization of the tax must be compared with the general spending pattern of the people. Thus, even for projects that are considered successful, the analysis must consider opportunity cost. When projects are designed to be implemented throughout India, there is a good chance that the project delivers a negative return. Even if the project delivers a net positive impact by itself, it can still be a net loss for the economy when weighed against the opportunity cost, which is if the tax money was not collected in the first place and the people were allowed to spend it themselves.

15

The Effects of a Centralized Education

Education policy is a contentious matter that has sparked debate across various issues. To make bold claims about the correct policy would be risky for anyone. However, it is important to address the issues in India and Mizoram without veering too far off the views of the 'education interventionists' and the 'aid pessimists' who favour laissez-faire.

Like many other countries, India has centralized its educational policy, just like its economy. The central government regulates the education policies of all the states. Criticisms of these ideas are mostly on the contents, and not on the basic premise of the concept itself. These criticisms are mostly confined to fixing minute details of the contents of these policies. However, the question of whether a National Education Policy should exist at all is rarely, if at all questioned. This is because citizens tend to have a subservient attitude towards a well-framed instruction from an authoritative figure. This general acceptance to policies and instructions is not confined to just education, but can be seen in all spheres of society, including non-government entities. This general perception is also evident within Mizoram. Discussions about education are confined to the policies of the government, the school curriculum, who or how the officers are and how the students are performing. There is an utter lack of discussion on whether the government should be involved in a school or a district at all, whether there should be a rigid curriculum, whether there needs to be a permit system at all or whether students need to undergo formal schooling in the first place. Even under the traditional education system, the headmasters of the popular schools were synonymous with their schools. This shows a need for autonomy and decentralization for improvement in education quality. In a country where there is an acute unemployment problem, it is crucial that the deliberations should be started from ground zero. There is a good probability that small tweaks here and there would not do much to get to the root of the problem.

People in their profound wisdom, put different types of blame on different stakeholders of the education industry; teachers of government schools are blamed for not putting in enough efforts and for trying to get postings in city areas only, private school teachers are blamed for running their schools as 'a business' and are only after profits, students are blamed for not really understanding their lessons which is the reason that they cannot get jobs, politicians are blamed for not implementing education policies properly and are not strict when it comes to transfers and postings. These exasperations are understandable, but they do not address the root of the problem.

Let us look at a very simple example to explain the situation that is plaguing the education system. Let us imagine a small village where there are various occupations. After some time, all the villagers start to flock to a particular occupation as it has become more desirable than the others due to various factors such as profitability and social status. One can quickly imagine what would happen in that village. The villagers would soon realize that flocking to a singular type of profession is not at all possible and without the intervention of an external agency, most of the villagers would soon migrate to other occupations as earning a little less is much better than not earning at all.

In a real-life situation, the interactions among various disciplines of study, the effects of a centrally mandated system of education enforced via regulations is much more complex, and the effects of any change is much more diffused, with each change taking a considerable amount of time to make a noticeable change but nevertheless, the effect is very much similar to this example. The government, with all its virtues, can never let people fail.

This intervention from the government does not end with just the curriculum, but it has its hands on the job market too. These interventions outside the schooling system further hide the fallacies which further lengthen the time for the effects to appear by spreading the redundancy in the supply of manpower to all the citizens in various forms, making its detection more difficult. Academic inflation has become a major problem over time as it is an unavoidable outcome of the over-supply in manpower in specific sectors.

One of the biggest ill-effects of a centralized curriculum, reinforced by a system of a centralized evaluation system, is that it leads to a mass race for attaining the top position. This competition, while necessary to a certain level, has many ill-effects when there are too many students chasing after the same goal, and it invariably leads to academic inflation. The variations we have are only among different subjects, but the job aims are more or less similar. In Mizoram, a majority of the students opt for the humanities streams, which are mostly confined to teaching and government jobs. Even among the hard sciences, the job aims are largely similar. This centralized system could be replaced by a decentralized system of learning where various institutions run after different goals such as placement, job security, a balanced life etc. If different institutions go after different goals, students competing for different goals can still have competition, but will be restricted to healthy levels. This hype for attaining the best result is also hampering the much needed look into the alumni of educational institutions.

The focus on year end results has also pushed the private schools to viciously produce toppers. The private sector, which is notoriously efficient in producing what the customer wants, grinds the hardest to produce the best results. Intellectuals often criticize these private schools for only chasing after grades. However, this is simply the private sector at work, which is to produce exactly what the customer wants; nothing more, nothing less. Hence, a government intervention which compiles performance data of the alumni of different institutions and publishes their achievements later in life will educate the consumer into making better choices.

The insurmountable challenge which comes with a centralized education system is that it requires an all-knowing entity to draft the policies, so as to bring out the best in each child, to accurately predict the job market of the future at least 20 years in advance and to accurately map all the racial, geographical and personal traits of everyone in the entire country. And as for students who might want to go abroad, the planner has to map all contributing elements of all available host countries.

The Dangers of Education for All

In an effort to bring about equity, better opportunity and also produce a civilized set of citizens for the future of the country, governments around the world have implemented an education system that can absorb people of all sorts, the rich and the poor and even people who are uninterested to partake. We have the belief that a standardized formal education brings a better quality of life for the citizens, which is partly true; but we often overlook the fact that it comes with new problems. A rat race is set in motion as people are not informed of the dangers of everyone running after the jobs provided by our formal education. While governments and educators do not explicitly advocate that everyone should try to attain the highest degree possible, the general perception of the public is veered strongly in this direction. Holding a degree also commands a certain level of respect from society.

Graduates have spent almost 20 years of their life in educational institutions by the time they attain their degrees. These institutions are mostly based on what was believed to help students have better opportunities in the job market and also apparently help them to make better choices in their life. We believe that education is the harbinger for all round development. However, we fail to see the trade-off when we commit 20 years of our life, chasing mostly the same thing as other people. The effect is that a majority of the people have traded off almost all other possible avenues with the hope of beating their competitors in the academic rat race. If we were to remove the emotion and look at this logically, the risk to reward would look bleak, especially for people who are not academically inclined.

Sparing a slight thought into this will reveal that the job market is not going to provide the type of skill that we have as it is similar with everyone else. To make matters worse, most of the students in universities and colleges are engaged in the humanities or the arts, which mostly provide teaching jobs to students who study the same discipline. Even in the science fields, many of the students are engaged in theoretical work. Theoretical work will only go so far when providing jobs for the students, just like the people in the humanities and the arts.

> ***The youth, who are victims of this wrong education system are also often blamed for not studying hard enough.***

While it is acceptable that a basic education is helpful for people to navigate their daily life, it is not right to assume that more academic education equals a better life, or an increase in intelligence. The government and the intellectuals need a serious introspection on the negative effects of academic inflation in Mizoram so as to reduce what we call under-employment. The New Education

Policy has tried to improve this by trying to stress upon vocational subjects. In fact, if we are serious about reducing unemployment, the vocational subjects must form the core of our studies and they must be continuously revised according to the market conditions.

16

The Keynesian Havoc

The Keynesian Theory came about after the economic crash of 1929 when the market seemingly failed to correct for the imbalance between the money supply and the demand for it. The market size kept on diminishing and the job providers were not hiring even when they required it. Moreover, labour costs did not go down beyond a certain limit and the prices also refused to go down beyond a certain limit. This was called 'sticky prices.' This was in direct contradiction to the price equilibrium concept. Thus, a new method of generating demand was proposed, which was government intervention. This opened the floodgates for printing new money as well as the acquisition of debt by governments. This theory was further affirmed by the Modern Monetary Theory.

India has been quite reluctant to reforms after the 1990 liberalization. It has been trying to lengthen the wave of this reform and has opted for quantitative easing. This has in turn led to an increase in non-performing assets due to business failures and scams, and has been a headache for quite some time. Mizoram is not an exception to this. The state governments in India, although unable to directly apply the traditional quantitative easing methods, often acquire debt through the Reserve Bank of India. Some states even resort to "off balance sheet" borrowings. Since spending is addictive, it needed to be checked. This birthed the Fiscal Responsibility and Budget Management Act. This law was kept in place to safeguard against irresponsible spending by the government. We have also maximized government spending by withholding payments such as provident funds, disbursements to contractors, delaying of withdrawals by departments etc. What has transpired in India has similar characteristics to the spending addiction that was also visible in other countries, which was in part attributable to the new concept that allowed for deficit spending. However, the true Keynesian spirit is often overlooked, which says that the nasty shock of the business cycle can be alleviated by increasing government spending during a business downturn, while during a business boom, taxes should be increased and government spending should be decreased.

The part of the Keynesian concept which says that government spending should be increased during an economic downturn is readily followed, but the part which says that government spending should be decreased and taxes should be increased after the economic recovery to build a war chest so that the government is ready for the next economic downturn is often conveniently ignored.

This has resulted in economic crashes in various countries; the very reason being the liberty granted to the, government for deficit spending. The government of Mizoram has also taken an advantage of this liberty, although it may not be very aware of the source of this liberty that is granted to it. This liberty has allowed for the expansion of government activities under all economic sectors, and availing central grants is seen as an important driver for economic development.

This enthusiastic spending has given the employees under the government a very high status in the society. Success is often measured by whether a person has qualified for a government job or not. The qualification granted by this concept has also allowed the government to continuously increase its liabilities towards its employees, so much so that it has become a burden to the government itself.

People are often not aware that the civil services that they highly cherish pose a huge liability to the government itself. Problems that creep up on any aspect of the economy are often blamed on the government for not doing enough, often failing to realize that problems can also be created because the government is doing too much. When these problems are identified, people like to blame corruption and the inefficiency of the government, which may be true. However, the solution which is often proposed that asks for a leader with angelic qualities is highly impractical. No one dares to ask the question,

'Should the government be involved in the first place?'. Moreover, whenever people ask for more government intervention, they fail to realize that the very act of asking for that action sacrifices their freedom in the process. The result is that we get a frustrated youth that cannot find opportunities within Mizoram.

The zealous government spending has also resulted in the absence of any safety cushion during a downturn. This was particularly visible during the economic haltage due to Covid. It may sound odd, but Mizoram was lucky that the contribution of the economic activities to government's revenue from within Mizoram itself was relatively small when compared to many of the other states or the jerk would have been felt to a much larger extent as Mizoram imposed lockdowns for a long time. Even so, the government coffers were so empty even after relaxations of the borrowing capacity by the central government that the state found it difficult to pay even the salaries of its own employees.

If an increased spending and a strong government presence was enough, it would create a lot of employment opportunities and would not put the state's economy in a vulnerable position. The spending, if it were having its intended effect, would create returns that would create a positive feedback loop, which would easily refill the economy with taxable transactions. It appears that creating an artificial demand that is not genuinely required by the market does not produce the same result as a spending which is urged upon by pure market forces. This is visible in the recent real estate problem finance in China orchestrated by firms such as the Evergrande

Group. Thus, I have to conclude that all spendings are not equal. A feature that is plaguing government spending is that it is often driven by political ambitions, and not the market forces. The interest groups that pressure the government into its spendings also often have objectives that are different from the main output of the spending. The money that is put into the market through these artificial demands can only consolidate itself in the form of inflation in the long run, if the money is not quickly absorbed by remittances into other states.

Even after Keynesian, the Market Is King

Somehow, people tend to believe that the market can be fooled, and that artificial demand can be created by channeling money into the state. Mizoram has been receiving a much higher sum of money from the Central Government than it remits. Revenue deficit grants have also been provided by the centre. Hypothetically, this would set the state on the correct fiscal path. However, the effect has been that the government has become a top-heavy entity, having a hard time channeling its resources for development purposes, and the standard of living has increased without the viable businesses to sustain it. This may make Mizoram unattractive for investors in the long run, which is highly undesirable.

People often blame corruption for the lack of a thriving economy in Mizoram. However, the ugly truth is that the heavy spending by the government has led the economy to something similar to the middle-income trap problem faced by some countries. Low-income countries that have come out of poverty face this problem as their attractiveness for investment goes down due to rising wages of their labor force. Mizoram is facing this problem even before undergoing an economic boom, as the income levels are propped up by enormous government spending.

Thus, the task of attracting businesses has become more difficult due to the non-alignment of the spending to market forces.

17

Fear of Financial Instruments, but Investing in Pyramid Schemes

Due to the misconception that is prevalent among the people of Mizoram, there is a misconceived fear of the stock market due to its dreaded 'crashes'. Data that is readily available from the internet also shows that per capita investments in the stock market from Mizoram are low, despite having a higher average income than many of the other states in India. Moreover, the Mizo society is deeply rooted into Christian ideals, which prevents people from overtly displaying the desire to achieve good investment returns. This subverted desire however, often displays itself as people who fail to educate themselves on investments are often duped into scams. The people of Mizoram would be far better off if they appreciated the safer channels of investment instead of denying that their wants exist. Investments other than bank deposits and post offices are mostly foreign to the general population. The people's mindset is also deeply influenced by the stability of government jobs, which provides job security for life. Any fluctuation or uncertainty in investment instruments such as equity are simply disregarded by the people. Scammers and manipulators often take advantage of this naivety by offering attractive investments with assured returns, which are often multi-level marketing schemes and scams.

What appears most far-fetched to the people of Mizoram is that a group of people can pool their money together, set up a company, hire an able CEO and achieve phenomenal returns.

This idea is as foreign to the people as getting a good return on a stock market investment. Instead, they prefer to place their bets on the phenomenal new idea of a person who can provide a 100% return within a year, with absolutely no risk. The police have unearthed huge ponzi schemes from people who appear to seemingly do not want 'material things' in their life. This hypocrisy is costing the economy of Mizoram dearly. Huge sums of money that could have been invested, provide job opportunities while providing handsome returns to the investors are wasted every year. People also like to make investments in the name of donations to religious based organizations such as The Bible Society of India. A belief also exists among the people that people who subscribe to the schemes of this Bible Society would be blessed with luck and prosperity, which, needless to say, is without any sound evidence. Even for other religious donations, people are influenced by one form of return or another, be it this life or the next. Hence, the people need to cultivate in their mind that expecting a return on an investment is completely natural and learning about the different instruments is not anti-spiritual.

Risk is also often seen as something that is out of the ordinary. So, any instrument which clarifies the risks associated with it is seen as something that people should stay away from. This mentality has pushed people into government jobs and government contracts, and the government has also tried to employ more people. A risk-free job appears very attractive to people. Thus, any source of livelihood that seems to carry risk is kept for the people who are unable to secure these types of jobs. The net result is that people who have the capability to manage risk successfully and create employment are captured by the salaried jobs. This leads to the lowering of the overall investment within the state. Investment culture is mostly non-existent, except for a few micro-entrepreneurs who have appeared recently. This lack of investment has also led to a very low tax collection base for the state government.

18

A Misconception on Value

Heavily interlaced with Christian values, the Mizo society holds a strong moral value on all aspects of societal life, including the economy. Yielding high profits is frowned upon in business. People regard high profit as a form of theft, especially in occupations where they believe they understand where the profit comes from; such as a fruit vendor, a meat sold by a butcher, or a vegetable sold in the market. This judgement gives way for some leeway when the product or service is looked upon as 'high class'; which includes the iPhone, the salary of an air hostess, or the profit made by a high- end restaurant. A failure to recognize that people pay for value and not the effort put in is often misunderstood. They claim that a daily wage laborer is not paid enough, but a business owner earns a lot of money doing next to nothing. The people often regard agricultural workers as being unfairly treated, while the vegetable sellers at the market that are not doing any of the production are reaping all of the profits. These misconceptions stem from the misunderstanding that payment is done by buyers for the perceived value that they get; nothing more, nothing less. When a person toils hard in the agricultural field, it does not entitle him to demand more money than what the buyer of that produce is willing to pay for. Demanding anything more through another agency such as a government does not only tamper with the market equilibrium, but is also a form of extortion. As heartless as it may sound, the tampering of the free exchange of produce for money just to help a person or a group of people would only reward inefficiency, or force a payment for a value which is not the true value of a commodity in a free market. Help should be provided in some other form, such as educating the farmer on how to produce more crops, properly market his produce or process his produce so as to make it more valuable. Providing help in the form of subsidies, free tools, free fertilizers, free irrigation, free pesticides or free seeds will only add to the problem, as more and more products that are undesired by the market are being produced, further reducing the market demand, and in turn the prices.

Any trade, including farming, requires freedom, including the freedom to fail. The very reason why government agencies tend to fail is also the reason why the agriculturists of Mizoram are stuck in poverty, as they both lack the freedom, or to face the difficulties due to failure and look for value in other areas. Complete failure presses upon the person to change his profession, which is bitter, but necessary. Help from any agency, be it a government or any other entity, should not be in a form which tries to manipulate market forces, but instead aligns the abilities of the beneficiary to it.

Since value is placed on material objects by most people, the concept that the same goods can become more valuable is not something that they can subscribe to. Thus, when agricultural products or land are resold by people on commission, these people are regarded as opportunists with little or no moral sense. However, these commissioners play a crucial role as they provide a link between the producer and the market. Just as speculators play an important role in the stock market, the commissioners also play an important role in linking the producer to the consumer. Their importance is reflected in the price the buyer is ready to pay for the goods sold on commission. If one thinks about it more deeply, most of the players in the market work for commission as they only move the product and do not make actual changes to it.

A Misunderstanding of Money

Money is no doubt an interesting subject. However, it is still regarded as a taboo by some people in Mizoram. Speaking openly about our earnings, our savings and our future money plans are not very common in Mizo society. At the same time, we still fall prey to the same scams that lure the supposedly greedier societies. Thus, it is clear that we are driven by the same motives as the people who are chasing their dreams of being millionaires. So, to shy away from what is so innate to human nature is not helpful for anyone. It simply results in docility towards scammers, prevents us from planning our financial future and makes us develop a certain hostility towards money related businesses.

Let us first discuss how money came into being.

First of all, it must be understood that money comes from surplus. This distinguished reader would be well aware that the barter system came into place, before a token form of money came into being. Even a barter system requires some surplus for it to function. A person who produces just enough is not going to trade with anyone else. It is only the surplus which is available for trade. Hence, surplus is the main reason that we have money. Money in the currency form was linked to the gold reserve of a country. This link was removed after the economic crash of 1929, and the fiat money system was then introduced. A fiat money does not have a value on its own, as it does not have a particular utility if it were to be used in its true form. Its value is derived from the belief that it will be accepted by other people as a form of exchange.

An economy that is without surplus does not have the requirement for money. A fisherman who catches just enough fish to sustain himself and his family does not have anything to trade. A farmer who grows vegetables and grains will first feed his family, and if there is no surplus, he would not trade with any other person of another profession. Trade exists only when there is a surplus. In the olden days, barter system was used. People simply traded their produce with other commodities. Wealth was limited to what was stored before it was damaged. The discovery of precious metals improved the wealth of the people by allowing them to store the products of their labor in other forms which are not easily perishable. These precious metals such as silver or gold allowed the storing of wealth which is not directly utilized by the owner himself, which can be said, is the beginning of a form of the modern currency that we have. Thus, the amount of wealth that a person can have has become virtually unlimited, in contrast to when wealth was restricted to the storing of useful items for later use.

When the modern money was initially printed, it was used as a substitute for the gold that was stored by a country. Therefore, a government could not print as much as it wanted. However, during the economic depression of 1929, bank-runs were so severe that the government was forced to move out of the gold standard, and brought in an era of fiat money. Fiat money does not have any physical backing. The only backing that it has is the promise of the government to pay an amount similar to what is printed on that piece of paper, whatever that value maybe. Therefore, modern currency is completely dependent on the ability of the government to regulate the amount of money in an economy. In India, the amount of money that is circulated in our economy is regulated by the Reserve Bank of India.

A common fallacy that I have often seen is the claim that money does not have real value. This fallacy is common in Mizoram, but to the defence of the Mizo people, it is also common all across the globe. This is not surprising because the concept of value, although appearing to be straightforward, is quite tricky to understand. When a common man thinks a little deeper, he quickly realizes that money is just a piece of paper, which is similar to any other paper, except for the fact that the government promises to do something about the figures that are printed on that currency. If and when the government fails, that value seizes to exist. This is true to a certain extent, but overlooks the fact that it is true for all commodities in an economy, including essential items such as food or clothing. Any commodity, including currency, can be traded, only to the extent that both parties accept that the future value of that commodity would be beneficial in one form or another. There is zero difference between essential commodities, luxury goods or even fictitious goods such as stocks or bonds in the marketplace. They are all regulated by the same concept which is the expectation that the commodity will deliver some value that would be useful to the buyer in the future. Trade only happens when this story is accepted by the parties involved in the trade.

Due to the misunderstanding of the value of money, the Mizo people often hesitate to discuss, learn or make plans about money. These taboo beliefs about money prevent people from educating themselves about money and securing their financial future. Even though people often hesitate to be actually focused on money, they are hit by the reality that money is a central and essential tool of the economy. Cash is simply a reward by the economy for ingenuity, hard-work and investment. Putting a taboo on the subject simply disables the population from improving their financial status. A person who saves money is not different from the person who toils hard in his farm as the end products are to both acquire value. Placing a pedestal on one and looking at the other in disdain is either hypocritical or fallacious. In economic terms, a person who works at the bank is in no way different to a person who rears cattle.

A Misunderstanding of Profit

Another misunderstanding that is common among Mizo people is that seeking higher profits, which in turn leads to earning more money is an act of greed. While the Mizo people believe this, they happily accept when a person has a higher income from a government or a corporation. I suspect the reason for this to be that it is more difficult to see the source of the money when the entity that is paying the salary is a large one. Small businesses that earn good profit are easier to judge as their size makes it simple to see the source of their revenue. Therefore, the Mizo people place small businesses in a different category, and do not grant them the moral freedom to charge more for their products. Moreover, when small business owners become successful, they are hardly congratulated while a person working in a government sector or a corporation or in sports is applauded when he earns a good salary.

When a person or a business entity is able to charge a good profit on any economic activity, it is due to the fact that that person or business is able to deliver value, and that that value is in demand, allowing it to be traded at a high profit. Therefore, contrary to popular belief, people should always look for higher profits, and try to make more money as the ability to make higher profit is a sign that the economy desires the product that is being delivered, as long as that economic activity is within the confines of the law.

What the Mizo people also fail to see is that even for a corporation to pay a good salary, it also has to make a good profit which equals taking money from his customers, in the same way that a small business owner takes money from his customer. In the case of a government, the money is taken forcefully from the people. Therefore, if any moral burden is to be placed on anyone, it should be on the government. However, the situation in Mizoram is that the smaller the entity, the higher the moral burden that is placed on that entity, which makes it very hard for smaller businesses and poor people to get themselves out of their financial difficulties. This misunderstanding of the flow of money in bigger institutions is a big hurdle for development. In fact, big corporations often have had good profit margins to get to where they are today at one point of time or another, even if their profit margins are not very large today. After they have achieved a certain size, they now have an advantage of economies of scale, which smaller businesses do not have. Therefore, judging smaller businesses that demand more money is anti-poor. Moreover, the value that is offered by smaller businesses is often misunderstood. They offer the flexibility that bigger corporations do not in terms of location, time of delivery, customer specific specifications et cetera. This flexibility requires more inputs from the business owner which costs money, and this cost is passed on to the customer. Customers who happily pay for the prices set by the small businesses when they are alone, are unhappy when they discuss it in various platforms as they compare the prices to that of large corporations.

At this point, the reader must be able to decipher that a misunderstanding of money is almost similar to a misunderstanding of what profit in an economy is. Money or any other commodity derives its value from its ability to trade in the market. Putting a certain commodity on a pedestal and downplaying the importance of another is an impediment to a full understanding on how the economy works. Calling a person who tries to earn money greedy or selfish, is similar to condemning who tries to obtain a better harvest from his cultivation. These two activities, although appearing to be very different to the people, are similar to the eye of the economist as they are both trying to obtain value.

19

Fallacies Surrounding Big Corporates

People have a natural tendency to be skeptical about entities that they do not fully understand. They fear that the giant corporations are out to get them, and can also be agents of foreign countries to infiltrate their home country. But the boring truth is that these corporations are not evil, and are neither pious. They are simply manned by humans who have the same ambitions as the fruit seller down the street. And just like other social institutions, they are also inflicted by corruption. However, the overall effect that they tend to cause is a rise in income and job opportunities.

This fear of big corporations is not localized to Mizoram, but is visible all around the world. Several taxes are imposed to reduce the alleged harm by these corporates. However, the countries that have the audacity to welcome these corporations tend to perform well in terms of development. Bangladesh has also seen a remarkable improvement during recent years after facing a lot of ridicule from other countries as being exploited by these multinationals, and is now being compared to India on several parameters. Vietnam has also garnered praise from the World Bank after switching to a market economy. In India itself, we have seen Gujarat adopt a similar model and is called 'Gujarat Model', while it is simply a market economy model. While corporations usually offer higher rates of labor compared to local markets, it is assumed that they decrease the rate of labor. Even in countries where the labor that they offer is said to be inhumane, they still provide a source of livelihood for the people who would be unemployed for a majority of the year. These people are often compared to developed countries, which is also a wrong thing to do as these laborers are offered these jobs for the same reason that they are willing to undergo these dangerous tasks at lower pay. If any comparison is to be made, it has to be with the conditions of life that these people had before they were offered these opportunities. If the offer is not better than their previous jobs, they would not take up the new job.

The pollution and decisions of corporations is also often questioned, and is not without cause. However, the notion that these corporations are out to get us is false. They are simply short sighted like the rest of us, as they are driven by the same people like us, who prefer to take a shortcut whenever possible. They are subject to market forces and also do good deeds when called upon. They also do a lot of research to reduce the harm on the environment. They do not only produce the wealth required to protect the environment, they have stopped the use of CFCs, they developed ways to safely dispose nuclear wastes, and developed bio-degradable plastics. They also do reduce wastage by devising efficient methods. Ultimately, they are controlled by the safety valve of people's decisions. The fact is that while they tend to grow to huge sizes, they are much safer than a big government as they always lack the force of law without the help of the government.

The swallowing up of local vendors by big corporations is also a fear that stems from a one-sided analysis. This is partly true as there is a shift in the economic opportunities when a new player enters the playground. However, people forget to look at the other side of the equation, which is the new jobs that are created.

Moreover, it appears that the new jobs are largely occupied by non-locals, which is also partly true. However, a look at various countries reveal that standard of living is improved when large businesses are present, which implies that the net effect is positive.

Just like other social entities, corporates also operate democratically. Decisions are based on votes. There are instances where the founders themselves are ousted from the company itself. The claim that the corporate system operates by helping the rich to stay rich is simply not true. Countries that welcome large corporations are often ridiculed, and is the basis of the fear of Mizo people. However, the evidence of this fallacy is visible in our next-door neighbor Bangladesh. They have faced a lot of ridicule for being paid meager sums while working in factories but they are now already competing with India in various development indices. People also try to pick and choose the type of jobs that are created. They do not want corporations because they feel that only low paying jobs are created. This is true to a certain extent but when you zoom out temporally, you can see that high paying jobs are created and the intermingling of the locals with the outsiders create an opportunity for the local players to adapt, as evidenced by the takeover of Jaguar Land Rover by Tata Motors, which would have been unimaginable during the economic liberation of the 1990s.

20

The Incorrect Assumption that Morality and Economic Soundness are Similar

The people of Mizoram often conflate moral ideas with economic principles. These moral principles, which vary widely even among a homogeneous group such as the Mizo tribe, are often very different from the actual principles of economics which are testable, falsifiable and make predictions on the outcomes. Religion, culture, geography, gender, race, history and a myriad of other factors influence the morality of a person or a community. So, to base the economic strategy on the moral values and even at times, the emotion of the community is arbitrary and would certainly lead to failure.

A good example of this phenomenon would be the prohibition of liquor in the state. The main reason for the prohibitionists is that the consumption of alcohol is evil according to the Bible. The anti-prohibitionists also try to justify drinking using the same book by quoting lines where drinking is allowed. Both sides of the debate miss a crucial point, which is to look at the evidence which is readily available from other countries, and also from within Mizoram itself. The important question to ask is which policy causes the least harm, as both prohibition and relaxation have their own ill-effects while having their own advantages. Thus, it is important to look at the trade-off while looking at any policy.

Another example for this would be the attitude towards illegal smugglers from the neighboring countries such as Myanmar and Bangladesh. People hold the firm view that the effects of the smugglers are evil and have a negative effect on the people. This is partly true, but it fails to look at the benefit of the trade that exists due to the smuggling. Since the benefits of trade are well-established, and do not require deliberation, it is completely fallacious to assume that the effects of a particular trade would have only negative effects on the economy. The ill-effect of this fallacy is that instead of looking at the illegal trades as an opportunity, people advocate for a stronger check on the illegal trades and hold a strong contempt against these businesses.

Economics is amoral. The impact of an economic activity is not affected by our assignment of moral values to it; it continues to do what it does with complete disregard for the feelings of the community. A policy which is completely in line with the moral values of the people would still wreak havoc on the economy if the policy is not economically sound. A conflation of righteousness and social justice with economic principles has led people to accept socialist and communist principles that are not economically sustainable. When people are more concerned with how things ought to be, rather than how things are, bad things happen. A closer look at how these socialist programs would be implemented quickly reveal that they are very often impractical. The saying **'sem sem dam dam, ei bil thi thi'** which tells us to share, is harmful when applied to large entities, such as a state. This concept of sharing has a profound effect on the economic model of Mizoram, and to place this concept under the scanner is almost blasphemous. However, for the sake of the future of Mizoram, it is necessary to do so. When sharing emanates from the heart, it does not harm and is useful for the society. Therefore, it works well in smaller units such as families, villages or small localities where the well-being of the participants are inter-connected. At this level, enforcement is not required. However, at a large scale, people will not only place themselves first but will also place the interest of the smaller units first, which is the reason why people tend to act unlawfully when it comes to redistribution of wealth. Thus, there is little or no moral burden for the perpetrator, while the act appears to be very corrupt for people who are not the benefactors. This brings about the need for enforcement of the sharing, which is often ineffective as the enforcers also have their own interests, which in turn leads to more checks, choking the economy as a whole.

21

The Economics of Theft

An analysis of the economics of a state or a country would not be complete without looking into the economics of theft. It would be easy to ignore theft while performing an analysis of the economy, but it would render the analysis to be incomplete if the role of illegal activities in the economy is ignored. The legality of an economic activity is irrelevant if one is to look at the benefits or losses occurring due to that activity. A wrong assumption is often made during discussions that activities which are outside the radar of the taxman is a loss to the state, which ignores the benefits derived from such activities for many families. Legal or not, any economic activity has a significant impact on the parties that take part in it directly or indirectly. Assuming that taxes that are not paid to the government are losses is also a very wrong assumption. Taxes that are not paid are also still a part of the economy; they are either spent or sit in a bank account, which form an asset for the bank. The only difference when taxes are not paid is who gets to spend the money. It is also fallacious to assume that a government would spend the money better than the person who had evaded the tax.

I find it crucial to understand that government policies and the assignment of what is right and wrong by the people has a direct impact on the type of illegal activities. There is also a difference in the values dictated by the institutions that control moral values to what is actually believed by not just the common man, but by the very members of that institution themselves. A good example of this would be the demand by the church to prohibit the sale of liquor. This divergence can also be seen in the dictated principles on how businesses should be run or on how people are supposed to behave while looking for employment, and how the people actually do behave. This dishonesty results in a very weak implementation of the laws resulting from these demands, which is often blamed on the weakness of the government. This dishonesty, should it arise from religious beliefs or from cultural practices, is bound to have its ill effects on governance. Thus, simply putting a blame on the government is not going to solve the problem. Also, simply blaming corruption and the lack of integrity of the executives is lazy. It lacks the application of a thorough analysis to identify the root cause of the problem. In the present example, the actual attitude of the people towards liquor is very different from the law. In a population where a very large portion of the people want to consume liquor, including some portion of people engaged in the enforcement itself, the result cannot be anything else other than a complete failure to eradicate the so-called social evil.

The Risks and Rewards of Theft

Before we discuss the topic further, I will try to explain the economics of theft for the uninitiated. Theft exists in all cultures in one form or another. Weighing the economics of theft on the risk to reward, we would see a very obtuse result. A thief spends almost nothing, but the profit is instant and almost always a hundred percent. It usually does not take a lot of skill, but the risk associated with it is abnormally high. While the reward is high and instantaneous, the risks can be incarceration, ostracization or even death. It is important to see the reasoning behind theft so as to truly see why people commit such crimes. Usually, a person who is already ostracized by society would have a lesser risk as compared to a person who has a high status in a society. Hence, we find that people who are not well integrated into the framework of society tend to commit petty crimes. In the case of corruption of government money, we see that people who have much to lose in terms of status often indulge in corruption, which appears to be an anomaly. This can be explained by the fact that the risk of getting caught is less, and that people who engage in corruption are not ostracized to the extent faced by a common thief.

The reward is also greater for corruption when compared to petty theft. So, what a thief does is weigh the benefit to the reward, just like any other businessman or entrepreneur.

The Economics of Corruption

My family loves the game of badminton. We tend to watch badminton matches whenever we find the time. At one time, there was a peculiar situation where the players were trying to lose, and were reprimanded for it. They were doing this because they had already qualified for the next round, and the losers would be able to face seemingly softer opponents. It was clear that corruption finds its way wherever it can.

Corruption has been a topic of interest for the people of Mizoram. Hence, let us place it under the microscope. In order to see why corruption is the most common form of theft, it is important to see the risk versus reward for engaging in corruption. People tend to engage in corruption mostly because the risk of getting caught is low in cases of corruption. In order to please the voters, the government implements various measures to prevent corruption. So, when corruption actually takes place, it is very difficult to pinpoint the exact point of lapse, or who has actually benefited from it as the people involved in the investigation or even the punishment of crimes might have a stake in the crime. The reward of corruption is also shared among many people, which whitewashes the crime in the eyes of the general public. Moreover, corruption imposes a lesser moral burden on the perpetrators, as the fund transactions are so lengthy that it takes a lot of financial analysis to even determine who has actually suffered due to the crime. The ill-effects are also dispersed, while the reward is concentrated. For example, let us look at a project which is implemented using funds that were received from the central government. The person who has benefitted from the corruption would simply increase the cost of implementation by some percentages, which is a very huge amount for large projects. The cost would be shared by the citizens of India, which means that it is very dispersed. However, the person who has committed the crime would receive a huge amount in a concentrated form.

This explains why the act of engaging in corruption imposes very little moral burden on the perpetrator. Moreover, the economy of a large country such as India is complex and its tax collection is so intricate that most people would not even bother to think about the complex flow of tax money. The manager of government money, be it the politician or the bureaucrat, is also not managing his own money. The ill-effects of inefficient usage hardly affect his income; and in the case of corruption, rewards him. Thus, even though the people of Mizoram tend to blame the lack of integrity and the lack of true Christianity, this moral hazard is a more likely reason why so many people engage in the crime of corruption.

Reducing Corruption

After understanding the reasoning of the thief, can we think about a way to reduce it? Should we say that it is an impossible puzzle to solve. I am of the opinion that this is true to a certain extent. However, I believe that it can be limited. First, let us look at how the moral hazard can be reduced. When the effects of corruption become so diluted that it becomes difficult to detect it instantly, it would be effective to shorten the chain of administration in the government. A city administrator could directly spend his city's tax money on the city itself. A village council could directly collect and spend money for the village itself. This would certainly shorten the chain and make corruption very visible. Moreover, there is an alignment of interest of the administrator to the project when the administrator belongs to the same locality. This would considerably reduce moral hazard. Thus, autonomy at all possible steps, clear cut delegation of responsibilities and a short money trail are crucial to reduce corruption. It has already been shown that creating excessive checks and balances only increases the number of people involved in corruption. Thus, making corruption visible is clearly more effective, just as the Right to Information Act has.

However, it is important to note that corruption can never be fully removed from a system where the managers are managing money that does not belong to them, are not objectively and immediately measured by the outcome of their spendings, and can tweak statistics or blame the predecessor government for the ills that have befallen the citizens. Thus, putting a limit on the functioning of the government is crucial to limit corruption. This point has not been stressed in the fora of Mizoram, which is unfortunate. Laws are often confined to what a government should do, but the part which says what it cannot do is often not given enough importance. The balance of power is so far tilted towards government agencies that the question that is often asked is how a government is not allowed to do something, rather than how a government has derived its power to do it. The government has taken a life of its own and tries to act on its own without asking the persons who are paying for its programmes. People often fail to question this as there is a lack of understanding that more power begets more taxes, which in turn breeds more corruption. People often blindly accept orders, even when those orders seemingly lack legislative sanction. The link between a powerful government, powerful in the sense that it has a lot of control over the lives of its citizens, to the level of corruption in that country might not appear so obvious, but there is a good correlation between them. All one has to do is look at different countries across the world. Countries that base their legislation on the freedom of the people generally tend to do better than those that surrender a large part of their freedom to their government in exchange for social welfare.[3] We must never forget that a government is a good servant but a bad master.

---

[3] Richard J. Cebula, J.R. Clark and Franklin G. Mixon, Jr., *The Impact of Economic Freedom on Per Capita Real GDP- A Study of OECD Nations* (USA: Jacksonville University, 2013), page 40.

The Black Market

The black market operates on a slightly different economics compared to normal theft or corruption in the sense that the person who engages in black marketing spends money to purchase the goods. Contraband goods are not free, as they also have an input cost. The input cost is transferred to the next seller, even if the item is illegal. Many of the contraband items seen in Mizoram were originally legal. A seller of illegal petrol would usually purchase the product from a licensed pump, and a reseller of subsidized rice would get it from a government retailer. The items become illegal when they are resold at market price. Other items such as exotic animals and narcotic substances would fall under a different category as some of them would be illegal from the initial point of the trade.

Let us focus on the items that were legal initially, and were later taken outside the framework provided by the government, as the selling of items that are well inside the acceptance of the society pose a lesser level of contention and therefore, require a closer look. These types of items typically are not harmful to the people, but are regarded as harmful to the economy as they are usually not taxed, are not sold as per rates specified by the government, are sold outside the place designated by the government or do not follow the quality prescribed by the regulatory bodies. These regulations are usually put in place when the item is scarce, is potentially dangerous or requires a certain level of expertise to determine its safety or quality. Selling above the Maximum Retail Price can also fall under this category as it is technically illegal to sell products above their marked prices. One could argue that some type of regulation is necessary to ensure a fair playing field for the participants of the market. This can be easily agreed as people need an entity to ensure their safety and their properties. They also need an authority who can punish cheaters. However, a problem arises when the control is excessive, is misplaced or goes against human nature. When this happens, the control itself becomes the very reason for the black market. Liberalists would argue that almost all government control is unnecessary. For example, the black marketing of liquor exists whenever there is a prohibition. This is not confined to Mizoram, but it can be seen in many countries. When prohibition is lifted, the black market disappears. The comparison should be between the ill effects of the prohibition and the free sale of alcohol, on which a lengthy debate could ensue. The case for control becomes even weaker when the substances are not harmful with proper use.

It is easy to blame the people who are taking advantage of regulatory orders and gain unhealthy profits due to these regulations. However, we must realize that society contains a spectrum of people; some possess the highest level of integrity, while on the other end of the spectrum, we may have some who are willing to do just anything to earn a buck. Having a system that rewards the people who are willing to break the rules is quite detrimental for any society. This is why strong criminal laws are always required to counter the side-effects of regulation, especially regulations that are not well positioned.

It is interesting to note that commodities such as petrol, diesel and LPG are openly sold in the black market of Mizoram. When such a situation exists, it is important to look at why people are so accepting of the black market. Maybe the regulation is too stringent, or maybe the reason is that the white market has failed the people in some other way. It is important to accept that whenever a black market exists, there is a gap in the white market which needs to be bridged. Having the humility to accept that our laws may need some tweaking, and in some instances, a major overhaul is important. Simply opting for a harsher punishment or strengthening the enforcement is a costly affair, and tends to backfire by inviting more corruption, as the very act of increasing the control provides more incentives to the law breakers. It is also important for Mizoram to see the black markets as opportunities, rather than ostracize these enterprises. People engaged in these types of trade would quickly move on to other things once they attain a certain level of wealth for new investment. Hence, the fear that relaxing restrictions would quickly increase the prevalence of undesired products is untrue, as people tend to self-regulate after a certain level. This is especially true in the case of the prohibition of alcohol, as the restrictions put in place by the government and the society does not seem to make much headway. Thus, the Mizo people must start to recognize that these not so welcome trades are also stepping-stones for people who are less fortunate, as the profit margins tend to be higher, while requiring lesser skills compared to other trades in the formal sector. Similarly, a sewage cleaner would easily earn a higher wage than a bricklayer, and a septic tank cleaner would easily out-earn an earth digger. The practice of banning people from engaging in dangerous work prevents people of lower income from improving their living standards. Methods that employ less intrusive means such as improving safety protocols would be more beneficial for poorer people.

The level of control and regulation also has an effect on the nature of crimes, the severity of the crimes and the morality in a country. Portugal had done away with the criminalization of drugs on the 29th, November, 2000 and instead focused on rehabilitation and care. The country outlined 13 strategic options to combat drug usage. Drug usage, drug related violence, deaths and diseases went down. This is exactly opposite to what most people in Mizoram believe. [4]There is a strong belief that harsher legal punishments and effective enforcement would bring the crime rate down. This assumption neglects the important 'economics of theft'.

Under prohibition, the profit margin of the illegal product increases by a considerable margin. Thus, it always finds a willing 'entrepreneur' who is willing to risk incarceration.

A harsher punishment would only increase the profit margin as the number of people who are willing to take the risk would decrease, thus decreasing the supply. Even

---

[4] Sonia Felix, Pedro Portugal, and Ana Tavares, *Going after the Addiction, Not the Addicted: The impact of Drug Decriminalization in Portugal* (Bonn, Germany: Institute of Labor Economics, 2017)

someone who argues for prohibition would have to accept that the prohibition would work only if it can be implemented. For example, let us imagine a scenario where the punishment is infinite i.e. death, the number of people who would be willing to undertake such a venture would drastically go down. However, it is extremely unlikely that such a law would be implemented in a society where the demand for such a product is very present, even if it were legislated. The chances of corruption would be high among the enforcement, the sellers, the consumers and even the judges if the gravity of the crime does not match the people's general attitude towards the crime. Thus, it would not be useful.

An understanding of the economics of theft would help the people of Mizoram while asking for legislation from its law makers, which makes it crucial that the people develop a habit of looking at the evidence available from other countries to come to a solution that is practical, is based in reality and not just rely on knee-jerk emotional reactions.

It is also interesting to note that economies that are freer tend to have less need to control crimes.[5] Socialist economies tend to have numerous laws to curb corruption. However, even after all the innovative checks and balances put in place, rampant corruption is usually visible. Amusingly, the situation that we are facing today is that the auditors of the government also need to be audited. This is due to the fact that the root cause, which

---

[5] Joshua C. Hall et al, *Economic Freedom and Recidivism: Evidence from US States*, (West Virginia University: College of Business and Economics, 2014).

is the incentive to commit corruption, is not removed. Rather, what has happened is that the people who are engaged in the checking of corruption have also come under suspicion. We tend to overlook the fact that the authority is also manned by people, people who are also flesh and bones, who are also affected by the same economy of theft and are also well capable of cheating. Just like a rotten apple spoils the whole basket, few people can ruin the system as the people who do not engage in corruption will be missing out on the action. People of high integrity would often not stop the people who are trying to engage in corruption, as these upright people stay away from corruption because they want to live a peaceful life, and would mostly like to stay away. Thus, socialist economies which contain higher levels of government control tend to have higher levels of corruption. On the other hand, capitalist economies tend to have lower levels of government corruption, simply because there is less opportunity for it. Private businesses simply cannot cheat on their business because they are managing their own money. Although unfair practices exist everywhere, cheaters are ostracized to a larger extent in a market economy as none of the players like a person who does not stand by his word. The businesses quickly gang up on the cheaters and they are swiftly discarded by a free market, thus reducing the need of an agency for control.

22

The Fallacy of Scale

It is difficult for the common man to imagine the scale of the financial problems that the government is facing. It is also difficult for a person who is not specialized in the subject to imagine the deficit of the income of our state to sustain our current living standards. Many people, including bureaucrats believe that reduction in the expenditure of the government on items such as vehicles, working lunches and official dinners can help alleviate the financial stress that the government is facing. However, when the state government collects only about a four-month salary of its employees from all of its tax and non-tax sources, and when it requires extra funds to the tune of about two thousand crores just to meet the salary of its employees, a reduction in the expenditure on items that are only a few crores, will do next to nothing to help the financial situation.

There is also a belief that our financial problem can be solved using simple methods such as the implementation of austerity measures in office expenditure, reducing corruption or improving farming methods. This stems from the mistake of not doing the necessary number crunching. In order to sustain our current way of life, private investments to the tune of thousands of crores is necessary. A few cuts here and there among government departments cannot alleviate the situation, as the number of departments in Mizoram multiplied by the cuts cannot amount to a large number.

The people also try to push the government to enable the people to be self-sufficient in food, especially rice as it is a staple food for the Mizos. They do this partly out of fear of being cut off from the mainland India, and also to save costs. However, the price of food, and especially rice has gone down drastically due to economic growth. The cost of rice is no longer a major expense for most families, and therefore spending time and money is futile. The focus must be shifted to spendings on healthcare, education and salaries of bureaucrats. There are also suggestions for the youth to take up low paying jobs to protect the economy, while failing to see that the money involved in this transaction is small. It is much more important to focus on the families that are on a tight budget to keep labor costs low than to worry about other factors such as preventing the cash from leaving Mizoram. Focus on small entrepreneurs is also important, but enough stress is not given to big investments. The people also have not placed pressure on the government to attract large investments. While small entrepreneurs also have the capability to grow into large companies, it takes time. It is much faster to attract large businesses, and try to provide opportunities for the youth in these businesses in terms of jobs or skills.

23

Fallacies Surrounding Entrepreneurship

Entrepreneurship is something which is not taught at a great extent in schools. Only people who are engaged in the profession or who go on to study business administration are familiar with the concept. There is a general misconception among the Mizo people that entrepreneurship is part of economy, and not the core of it.

Most Mizo people believe that integrity, having faith in God, or a government that is free of corruption are the ingredients for establishing a society that is pleasant to live in. However, it is important to look at how people acquire their values and their religion by looking at their socio-economic background. For our example, we can look at the Mizo people who were born and raised in different places. Mizo people who are born within Mizoram often have similar value systems while the very Mizo people who are born outside Mizoram seem to have a slightly different sets of values. Man by nature, has empathy, and it can be assumed that a person who has enough will have a certain inclination to help other people. This assumption of course excludes sociopaths and people with certain personality traits that fall outside the generally believed normal psychological characteristics. Therefore, the difference among the Mizo people who were raised elsewhere can be attributed to the social and environmental factors. Thus, trying to build a society that comprises citizens who are full of integrity, and charitable while ignoring entrepreneurship when the society consists of people that are poor could be a difficult task to accomplish.

Entrepreneurship develops the economy, and therefore allows people to show their empathy and is therefore an important ingredient in the establishment of a society that is pleasant to live in.

The belief that entrepreneurship is not the core of the economy harms Mizoram economy much more than what even the people who are educated in economics believe.

This misunderstanding has let people base their economic activities around other things such as equality, upliftment of the poor, social justice, and other good sounding phrases.

Although these good sounding phrases have good intentions behind them, they do not yield desirable results. What separates man from other animals is his ingenuity. Yuval Noah Hararri, author of Sapiens and a renowned historian had rightly said that the enterprising nature of man is what allows man to separate himself from all of the other species and dominate the planet. A surprising thing about humans when compared to other species is that humans are not the most efficient when it comes to using their energy to travel large distances, if we were to do it without any of the modern technology. However, if you add a bicycle to the equation, mankind surpasses all the other species by a tremendous amount. The bicycle is possible only through the enterprising nature of humans. Thinking about it from our vantage point today, inventing a wheel and creating a bicycle does not carry risk. However, if you think about a man who had to plant his crops and hunt for his food, it was very risky. The pursuit of the creation of a bicycle, which may or may not help him in the long run, could lead to him missing his meals. Thus, the risk taken by an entrepreneur is very real and the loss of a significant amount of time and resources remain an ever-present danger. When society does not nurture this risk-taking mentality, the people will surely fall back to their default state, which is to play safe and go by what they have today and try to continue as long as possible.

In a state like Mizoram, which is a part of a country with socialist ideals, the concoction of the socialist idea with the moral values of the people, which tends to downplay the goal of an entrepreneur, which is to acquire wealth and achieve financial independence has a very profound effect of discouraging its people from pursuing enterprising endeavors.

There is also a strong belief that the lack of natural resources such as oil or gas is one of the impediments for the development of the state, while evidence shows that countries that are devoid of natural resources can become rich, and countries that have an abundance of natural resources also remain under abject poverty.

People are mostly inclined to take up government or corporate jobs. Amazingly, people are not discouraged to pursue careers in sports. This may be due to the reason that sports is somehow linked to patriotism. However, success is ultimately based mostly on getting a government job, and the sportspersons are usually given government jobs when there is a belief that they have attained enough prominence.

Even though statistics reveal that poorer states in India such as Bihar tend to do well in central government job recruitment, people still believe that qualifying for jobs under the Government of India is an indicator of progress instead of looking at the data around business entrepreneurship. This is partly fueled by the belief that bureaucrats hold a considerable amount of power and the Mizo tribe could perish without Mizo officers holding these bureaucratic jobs. This could be a result of a lack of proper understanding of Indian polity by the Mizo population. The real rules of power and the negotiating power of states in India appears to be beyond the grasp of the common man.

The people's value system which places entrepreneurship below the government recruitments is one of the major hurdles for the economic growth of Mizoram. The people believe that bureaucrats, who spend money which was forcefully taken by the government from the people through taxation are more noble than people who run legit businesses, which can take money only from willing customers, and these customers will only continue to trade with that business only if the value that they get from the trade exceeds the amount that they pay for the product or service.

Due to the placement of entrepreneurship and businesses at a level lower than government activities, religious activities and non-government organization activities, the government and the society do not hesitate to take swift action on businesses that cross the accepted line set by the society. For example, food trucks were banned by the local people, claiming that these food trucks were inviting undesirable activities in their vicinity, without considering the option of increasing police presence in these areas. Also, people are not allowed to open their businesses on Sundays as most Mizo Christians worship on Sundays. The people are also expected to be present for church service on Saturdays and hence are expected to close their shops early because faith comes first. On the other hand, a police officer on duty is given a free pass even if his work falls on a Sunday as his job is considered important. Moreover, a business owner is not expected to talk about his profits and show his earnings as people consider it to be impolite, while it is perfectly okay for the government servant or an executive of a large corporation that people deem to be important to throw a party for his promotions.

If the ultimate goal of a career is considered sinful, superfluous, and do not contribute to the well-being of the people, we would not find youngsters jumping in to risk a significant duration of their lives as well as a large amount of resources.

These attitudes, although appearing to be subtle, have significant impacts on the spirit of entrepreneurship in Mizoram.

This does not seem to be disappearing soon, but changes can be seen. Mizoram has seen new innovations in the field of food processing, baking, fashion, online businesses, and other small-scale industries. These small breakthroughs are significant, and force people with traditional views to incrementally change their stand.

People without an understanding of the importance of human ingenuity will point to other things such as lack of natural resources, insufficiency in the production of food, lack of self-sustainability or lack of industriousness among the people. They will point to other countries and will find evidence to support their views, as statistics can be contorted easily to suit one's needs. The lack of actual number crunching leads people to believe that self-sufficiency in food grains is the most important thing for the people of Mizoram, while forgetting that India already produces a surplus of food grains, thus exporting it. This mindset, which tries to sustain a living, but does not try to grow the economy is common in Mizoram.

A lack of understanding of the difference between value addition and simply producing a product is a major impediment to the understanding of the true value of entrepreneurship. A chunk of metal cannot do much, and is not worth that much either. However, when that metal is turned into a useful product, such as a knife, it becomes a tool to grow the productivity of the person wielding it.

One interesting phenomenon that occurs after wars is that the economy tends to shoot upwards soon after the wars end. However, to a person who understands the value of human ingenuity, and the value of a set of people who are skilled to do specific jobs and come up with a product, this phenomenon is not surprising at all. The simple fact is that at the end of the war, the people who were there in the country before the war, are still the same people. The destruction of infrastructure by the wars did not take their skills away. These people know exactly what it takes to come up with a product and how to execute it and therefore, it takes no time to rebuild what was broken. This should be an example of how important entrepreneurship is, as entrepreneurship is the only way to learn new ways of doing things and come up with new products by adopting new strategies. This fact also disproves the claim that the lack of growth in an economy is a result of lack of infrastructure or lack of money.

The concept of value addition and how it operates is also often misunderstood by bureaucrats, who are supposed to be mostly educated. When an entrepreneur adds value to a certain commodity, and he sells it at a much higher price, bureaucrats tend to blame the entrepreneur. They believe the entrepreneur is exploiting the producers. These bureaucrats still hold the traditional view that the producers who do the most valuable job should be compensated fairly. However, the market does not lie.

It is simply not prudent to pay a large sum of money for a commodity, which one can easily produce on his own, even if that commodity is food. This view is held by the bureaucrats, holding the spirit of entrepreneurship back by putting burden on the people engaged in taking risks. The risk that is taken by entrepreneurs is not incorporated by the bureaucrats and therefore, their prices look exploitative to them.

24

The Scrooges of Christmas

Although this perception is similar to the fallacy around price control, it is necessary to discuss it as it is peculiar in some ways. The businessmen of Mizoram are given bad names for not giving Christmas discounts. People say that they take advantage of the rural people who have come for Christmas shopping to Aizawl. They compare them to the big brands and the businessmen in other states who give flashy discounts during Diwali. Christians are supposed to be more altruistic, so what could be the reason?

It is easy to fall into a fallacy of comparing things that look similar, but different upon a closer look. It may look completely logical to people to compare the Mizo businesses to the businesses in other states and the big brands. However, a closer look will reveal the small but significant differences that make them behave in the opposite manner.

Places of tourist attractions tend to have higher prices. Festivals also tend to jack up prices. This phenomenon can be attributed to people going on spending sprees during these occasions, among other factors. This could be the reason why we do not get discounts like other places during the Decembers in Aizawl, as Aizawl temporarily behaves like a place of tourist attraction for the other districts and the villages, coupled with the festive spirit of the customers during the season and lesser competition due to restrictions. Hence, the Scrooges of Christmas have a reason to be scrooges.

Places that have an oversupply of businesses, as well as brands that use strategic discounts tend to offer discounts to boost their sales. These businesses behave in a different manner because they have plenty of competitors, and the locations of their businesses are usually not places of tourist attractions. Brands also do not offer discounts without proper planning. They display attractive discount rates, but the bigger discounts are usually on older items and goods that do not sell well. Therefore, a side-by-side comparison without looking at the differences will lead to wrong results.

25

The Evils of the Anointed

Due to the nature of religion, which is to exterminate all evil and all wrong- doing, the people in Mizoram have the mindset that all undesirable social elements must be completely removed. This has let them devise plans and ideas that are detrimental to economic growth and hamper opportunities for people of lower economic status. For example, people want the prohibition of all types of immoral things that appear in the Bible such as drugs, alcohol and even prostitution. This desire to completely remove antisocial elements has symptoms in other areas that are not visible to these people. A reason for the apparent correlation between the prevalence of drug abuse with respect to rate of economic growth, and subsequently to the availability of leisure time as well as increase in the disposable income can be drawn. With economic growth, the people have free time, and also look for various forms of entertainment, as these are the people who had previously been confined to work, or are guided by the mentality of their parents who were compelled to work daily. This transition period is one of the reasons for the wide usage of drugs. The people are quick to blame this on evil and the declining social morality. However, we have seen a decrease in the usage of drugs and other intoxicants in Aizawl as the people have adapted to the change, while it is still a problem in the suburbs of Aizawl as well as in the other districts, where the people have not adapted fully. Not much time has passed since the people of Aizawl were alarmed at the usage of drugs and the spread of AIDS, and that it would wipe out the entire Mizo community. These alarmists have called a ban on all types of intoxicants that they deem undesirable and that the only solution is to totally exterminate these evils. These people close their eyes to the reality that is evident in all parts of the globe, that at least a small portion of the community tend to indulge in one form of intoxicant or the other. They close their eyes to the fact that even the most advanced economies still fail in their war on drugs, and not even bother trying to ban alcohol. This fallacy stems from the idea that what is bad must be completely removed. This may be true for an individual, but it cannot be said the same for a community or state, which consists of individuals with different desires, ambitions and ideals. I completely agree that many things that humans indulge in are undesirable, but just as it is illogical to devote the entire GSDP of Mizoram in the fight against a skin disease, I find it illogical that the state should keep spending so much of its time and energy on removing the bits and pieces of the supposed evil that exist, will continue to exist and are subject to various forces which we do not fully understand.

26

Press Freedom and Democracy

While we often discuss the importance of the freedom of the press, we fail to see that freedom can only exist when there is financial independence. The Supreme Court of India has also rightly said that the independence of the judiciary does not mean anything if it does not have financial independence. In a country like India, the government has a deep control on almost all sectors of the economy, and therefore it also has considerable control on the money-making power of the press. In Mizoram, there are only a few players as the market is small. The journalists of Mizoram also do not make much owing to the market conditions prevailing in our state. With good intentions, there is a general support from the public, the journalists themselves and also the government on the idea that journalism should be promoted by the government. A term called 'accredited journalist' exists in Mizoram. These journalists obtain several facilities from the government such as travel facilities and other forms of financial help. Many newspapers in Mizoram also obtain advertisements from the government, apparently not due to the need of the government but as a form of help. These appear to be harmless. However, a closer look will reveal a dangerous slope that the state could slide into. As long as the press is connected to the government, and the press see the government as a source of their livelihood, we cannot expect them to bite the hand that feeds them. Lately, there are pressures for the creation of pension schemes for journalists. If this is done, the journalists will be or will hope to be on the government payroll. A master-servant relationship will soon ensue, which is highly undesirable as democracy cannot function without a free and independent press. If the fourth pillar of our democracy does not have sufficient independence, the main aim of this book, which is to orient the economy to the market to a greater extent, will never materialize.

27

Fallacies Around Agriculture

The Economic Survey of Mizoram for the fiscal year 2023-24 shows that agriculture and allied activities provide more than 50% of employment for Mizoram, while the percentage contribution to the Gross Value Added is only 25.23%. Thus, it is clear that people engaged in the agriculture business earn very less. The reader may find it odd that I have put the term 'business' after 'agriculture', which is the exact problem that I am trying to address. The people of Mizoram, much like the people from the other states of India, hold the view that agriculture is too important to be commercialized. The belief that is held by the people irrespective of the market value of agricultural products has allowed heavy interference of the government on the sector. The term profit is deemed to be inappropriate when it comes to food. The emotions of the people are especially volatile when it comes to rice, as it is a staple crop. Talks about the dangers of the food supply to Mizoram being cut-off are common. This has led people to believe that Mizoram has to self-sustain on food and other essential commodities. The improvements in road and air connectivity are ignored by these people. Moreover, the most fundamental root of economics, which is that people want to exchange their goods for money, is ignored. In this day and age, even if some sellers refuse to sell to us under exceptional circumstances, there are ten other sellers waiting to replace them. Even if the new sellers sell to us at a slightly higher price, it would still be much cheaper than trying to produce everything that we need. Thus, investing in an event that will not occur during the foreseeable future is pointless.

Mizoram has seen a number of government schemes to boost agricultural production but many people are frustrated that the farmers are still poor and blame the government for their situation.

However, the fact is that there is absolutely no shortage of food in Mizoram, and the poverty of the farmers is not due to lack of help, but due to lack of commercialization. Any sane person would laugh at a businessman who opens a shop without figuring out what his profit margin is going to be. However, the people are still pressing the government to help boost the production of the farmers, sometimes leading to huge piles of crops being left to rot. The only justification is that food is important, and the growers need to continue planting their crops for the next year. Thus, the only way out of this mess is to call a spade a spade and treat agriculture as what it actually is, a business, and the farmers should approach it as such.

28

Conclusion

People under democratic governments are often unaware of the power that they hold. They are frustrated and complain that democracy is flawed. Yes, it is true that it is flawed, but it really does confer a lot of power to the voters. It is by far the best system that we have. The biggest hurdle that a democratic system faces is that the voters cannot clearly see the outcome of their choices at the macro level. This is because the overall effect of individual choices does not necessarily equal the sum of its parts. This is where the right method of thinking is crucial. A population behaves differently from an individual, and it must be treated as a separate organism altogether, just like we tell people as individuals to save, but we try to boost spending at the macro level. Some phenomena are so counterintuitive that we fall for the same fallacy over and over again. People need to be informed that they are prone to fallacies if they do not put their biases aside and look at the facts, however uncomfortable that may be. Placing blame on others is easy, but putting the blame on oneself is difficult. To place blame on oneself for the slow growth of the country is impossible, if one does not put belief and faith aside and look at the facts for what it is. The discourse within this book was aimed towards making one question oneself. If there was any sort of success in its aim, I strongly believe your prior understandings must have been questioned. And if there was enough inspiration, the points made within this book itself must have been questioned and the correctness must have been verified with the reader's own collected evidence.

29

Bibliography

Banerjee, Abhijit V. & Esther Duflo. *Poor Economics*, Random House India, 2013.

Cebula, Richard J., J.R. Clark and Franklin G. Mixon Jr. *The Impact of Economic Freedom on Per Capita Real GDP- A Study of OECD Nations,* Jacksonville University, USA, 2013.

Graham, Benjamin. *The Intelligent Investor, Harper and Brothers*, 2017).

Dodsworth John R., Erich Spitaller, Michael Braulke, Keon Hyok Lee, Kenneth Miranda, Christian Mulder, Hisanobu Shishido, and Krishna Srinivasan. *Vietnam Transition to a Market Economy,* Washington DC: IMF, 1996.

Keynes, John Maynard. *The General Theory of Employment, Interest and Money*, Atlantic Print Services, 2023.

Felix, Sonia, Pedro Portugal and Ana Tavares. *Going after the Addiction, Not the Addicted: The impact of Drug Decriminalization in Portugal,* Bonn, Germany: Institute of Labor Economics, 2017.

Friedman, Milton and Rose Friedman. *Free to Choose*, Harcourt, 1980.

Hall, Joshua C., Kaitlyn Harger and Dean Stansel. *Economic Freedom and Recidivism: Evidence from US States*, West Virginia University: College of Business and Economics, 2014.

Harrari, Yuval Noah. *Homo Deus (A brief History of Tomorrow)*, Harvill Secker, 2016.

Hayek, FA. *The Road to Serfdom,* Routledge Classics, 2017.

Ratna, Lindawati Lubis. *Assessing Entrepreneurial Leadership and the Law: Why are these important for graduate students in Indonesia?* Indonesia: Telkom University, 2017.

Sowell, Thomas. *Economic Facts and Fallacies.* Basic Books, 2011.

The Economic Survey of Mizoram, 2023-24. Government of Mizoram.

www.ingramcontent.com/pod-product-compliance
Lightning Source LLC
LaVergne TN
LVHW041947070526
838199LV00051BA/2935